THE WORST
DAY I EVER HAD

THE WORST
DAY I EVER HAD

By Fred McMane and Cathrine Wolf
Illustrated by Brad Hamann

A *Sports Illustrated For Kids* Book

First Edition

Library of Congress Cataloging-in-Publication Date

McMane, Fred.
    The worst day I ever had/Fred McMane and Cathy Wolf.—1st ed.
        p. cm.
    "A sports illustrated for kids book."
    Summary: Thirteen prominent sports figures, including Martina Navratilova and Magic Johnson, tell of their biggest blunders and heartbreaks and how they managed to recover and go on to greater glory.
    ISBN 0-316-55354-9
    1. Athletes—Biography—Juvenile literature. 2. Disappointment—Juvenile literature. 3. Achievement motivation—Juvenile literature. [1. Athletes. 2. Sports. 3. Disappointment.]
I. Wolf, Cathy. II. Title.
GV697.A1M37 1991
796'.092'2—dc20
[B]   91-14765

Sports Illustrated For Kids Books is an imprint of Little, Brown and Company.

10 9 8 7 6 5 4 3 2 1

WOR

For further information regarding this title, write to Little, Brown and Company, 34 Beacon Street, Boston, MA 02108

Published simultaneously in Canada by Little, Brown & Company (Canada)

Printed in the United States of America

Cover and interior design by Pegi Goodman

DEDICATION

To our mothers, Meta McMane and Marian G. Wolf; to the memory of Maria Wolf and Margaret Gregory; and to all the other "wise women," living and dead, who have helped us face our worst days with faith, hope, and humor.

CONTENTS

ACKNOWLEDGMENTS

Our thanks and appreciation, first of all, to the folks at SI For Kids Books, Neil Cohen, Mary Morel, and Margaret Sieck, for conceiving this project, giving us the chance to execute it, and then putting up with us, through the worst days and the best.

Thanks also to the journalists, public relations directors, and other helpful individuals who enabled us to get the atheletes' stories. Annisa Mansour of the JJK Foundation, Susie Mathieu of the St. Louis Blues, and Susie Akos of IMG were especially patient and perseverent in the face of increasingly frantic phone calls.

Most of all, though, we would like to express our deep appreciation and thanks to the athletes who shared so generously of their time, their thoughts—indeed, parts of their lives—in telling us these very personal stories. Without their gracious participation, there would be no book.

INTRODUCTION

ave you ever had a bad day? You know, one of those days when things seem to go all wrong. Maybe you made a big mistake. Or maybe you were badly disappointed by someone or something. Or maybe something terrible happened to you. Whatever it was, you probably felt as if it were the worst day you had ever had. And you probably felt that you were the only one in the world who had ever had such a bad day.

Guess what? You weren't alone.

Everyone makes mistakes and experiences disappointments at some point in his or her life. Even great athletes have bad days.

That's what this book is about. We asked 13 of the world's finest athletes a similar question: What is the worst day you ever had? Their answers are as varied as the sports they play. Some of their stories are from the playing field; some are not. Several recall tragic, even life-threatening experiences; other report dis-

appointment, injury, and defeat. One, swimmer Shaun Jordan's worst day, is just plain embarrassing.

Surely, the life of a star athlete is filled with great days—the days you read about in magazines or see on TV. But just like you, almost every star athlete has had bad days. Cyclist Greg LeMond and race car driver Shirley Muldowney suffered accidents that left them near death. Hockey star Brett Hull and pro basketball player Willie Anderson got cut from teams they really wanted to play on. Tennis pro Martina Navratilova lost a match that she thought meant the end of her career, and pro hoops star Karl Malone faced an academic problem that did end his career—temporarily.

But as a wise woman once said, "It's not what happens to you in life that counts, it's how you handle it that really matters." When Karl was told that he wouldn't be allowed to play basketball in college because his high school grades were so bad, he was scared and upset. He almost decided not to go to college at all! But with help from his family and friends, Karl learned from the situation. He worked hard to improve his grades and went on to be a success, both in the classroom and on the court. Karl's worst day was a turning point in his life that made him a better, stronger person.

All the athletes in this book learned something from their worst days. And their examples give the rest of us hope— hope that we, too, might look at our bad days and figure out what they can teach us. For, in fact, every bad day has more to offer than tears and disappointment. If we can grab the good that a bad day has to offer, we might discover that, most of the time, things really can work out for the best.

CHAPTER 1

WILLIE ANDERSON

Now an NBA star, Willie was an early cut at his first team tryout

Willie Anderson, the San Antonio Spurs' high-scoring guard, has had plenty of good days on the basketball court. Ever since high school, he has averaged double figures in scoring on every team he has played for—including more than 17 points per game since joining the National Basketball Association in 1988.

As a senior at the University of Georgia, Willie scored an average of 16.7 points per game and was named to the All-Southeastern Conference team. In 1987, he played on the U.S. basketball team that won a silver medal at the Pan American Games in Indianapolis, Indiana. The next year, he won a bronze medal as a member of the U.S. team that played at the Summer Olympics in Seoul, South Korea.

Willie was the 10th player chosen in the 1988 NBA draft. He earned NBA All-Rookie honors in 1988-89 when he averaged 18.6 points per game, second best on the Spurs' all-time rookie list. He also made more steals (150) than any rookie in the team's history, and finished second in points (1,508), assists (372), and minutes played (2,738).

In the 1989-90 regular season, Willie played in every Spurs game,

13

averaging 15.7 points. In the play-offs, he averaged 20.5 points, to help San Antonio win a post-season series for the first time in seven years.

Willie's cool, graceful moves toward the basket remind San Antonio fans of former Spurs star George Gervin. George was called Iceman, so the fans nicknamed Willie Chill.

Willie remembers that his basketball career didn't begin so smoothly. The worst day Willie ever had took place in the fall of 1979, in his hometown of Atlanta, Georgia. Willie was 12 years old, and he almost gave up basketball forever.

had always enjoyed playing basketball, and for a long time I looked forward to the day I could play on a school team. I thought I would get my chance in September 1979, when I started going to a new school, East Atlanta High.

My old school, H.O. Burgess Elementary, only went through the seventh grade. East Atlanta started at the eighth grade. It was a big school that took kids from a lot of neighborhoods. Most of my classmates at H.O. Burgess went to another high school, but my parents and I chose

East Atlanta, even though it was all the way across town. We just liked it better.

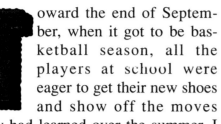Toward the end of September, when it got to be basketball season, all the players at school were eager to get their new shoes and show off the moves they had learned over the summer. I was excited because there was an eighth-grade team at East Atlanta, and I really wanted to play on that team. I had worked hard on my game over the summer, and I was confident that I could make the team.

When tryouts began, I realized that most of the other kids were totally new to me. They had come from different elementary schools. But I also noticed they were not so new to the coaches, who were familiar with the students who lived close to the school. There were only a few kids from H.O. Burgess trying out for the team, and we began to think that we might be in a bad situation because we came from across town.

I decided I'd just have to play better than those other kids to get the coaches' attention. I probably tried

DURING TRYOUTS WILLIE PLAYED THE BEST HE COULD.

THE COACH HARDLY GAVE ME A CHANCE. I NEVER WANT TO PLAY HOOPS AGAIN.

CUT LIST

too hard on that first day of tryouts. I didn't play poorly, but I didn't do anything fantastic. Some kids made one or two great plays; I was just steady and solid. But I was also a five-foot-three guard who was shorter than many of the others.

I was cut after that first day.

I felt devastated. I wanted to play for the orange-and-blue Wildcats so bad! Being cut hurt, but it hurt even more to be one of the first players to be cut. In fact, all my friends from H.O. Burgess were cut. I felt I never had a shot at making the team.

The head coach, William Pierce, told me that he had a lot of guards who were better than me. But I felt that I hadn't been given a chance to show him what I really could do. How could he tell that other players were better when he only gave me one day to prove myself? I was sure it was favoritism: I had been cut because I came from the other side of town! I became very depressed.

I went right home and talked to my parents about how I felt. They picked up my spirits a little bit. My mom said I would become a better player if I

WILLIE WENT HOME AND TOLD HIS PARENTS HOW DISAPPOINTED HE WAS.

QUITTING ISN'T THE ANSWER. YOU NEED TO WORK ON YOUR GAME SO YOU'LL BE READY FOR NEXT YEAR'S TRYOUTS.

MY PARENTS WERE RIGHT ABOUT THIS REC LEAGUE. I'M AVERAGING 20 POINTS AND 10 REBOUNDS A GAME!

NEXT YEAR, WILLIE MADE THE NINTH GRADE TEAM AND HAD HIS BEST SEASON EVER!

WILLIE'S HARD WORK HAS MADE HIM ONE OF OUR BEST PLAYERS.

continued working at my game. I listened to what she said, but I still felt terrible. I didn't play basketball for two months because I was so upset about what had happened. I thought I might never play basketball again.

The next summer, my parents talked me into trying out in the Samuel L. Jones Boys Club Recreational League, in Atlanta. I played really well and averaged more than 20 points and 10 rebounds per game. Coach Pierce often came out to watch the summer-league games, and he recognized me. That made me play even harder, because I wanted to get back at him, to show him how good I was.

hen school started in the fall of 1980, I didn't want to go out for the ninth-grade basketball team. Coach Pierce was helping Coach Judson Grant with the team, and I was still angry and very rebellious. I figured I would wait another year and then try for the high school varsity team instead.

But the varsity coach, George Gray, said I should go out for the ninth-grade team. I finally agreed, and guess what? That turned out to be my best year ever in basketball! I averaged 26 points, 10 rebounds, and five assists. I also loved the competition and the opportunity to represent my school. It was a great year!

I learned a lot of lessons from my worst day. Being cut taught me that when you fail, the only thing to do is improve. Some athletes are blessed with natural talent, but I wasn't. Once I faced that fact—instead of blaming my failure to make the team on the coach—I realized that I could either quit or work hard to improve my game. I decided to work hard, and I have never regretted that decision.

Some of us need disappointments to help build our character, both as people and as athletes. I feel that dealing with that big letdown when I was 12 years old helped me learn to deal with letdowns later in my life. After all, I found out that one disappointment doesn't mean it's the end of the world!

CHAPTER 2

BRETT HULL

After a fast NHL start, Brett was blindsided by a trip to the minors

rett Hull is the National Hockey League's newest superstar. After years of struggling with having a famous name and an easygoing attitude, Brett came into his own during the 1989-90 season. He lit up the league in 1990-91!

But being a late bloomer isn't easy when your sport is hockey and your dad was one of the greatest hockey players ever to lace up skates. Bobby Hull, Brett's father, played for the Chicago Blackhawks, the Winnipeg Jets, and the Hartford Whalers from 1957 to 1980. His smooth skating and lightning-fast slap shot helped him score 50 or more goals in a season nine times.

Brett was born in Ontario, Canada, in 1964 and got his start when his dad strapped skates on him at age 3. As a kid, Brett became great at shooting the puck, but at 17, he almost quit the game because none of the junior teams, which serve as a training ground for future NHL players, wanted him.

Luckily, Brett got a tryout with a junior team in Penticton, British Columbia, and made the club. Then in the 1983-84 season, he scored 105 goals in 56 games! In 1984, Brett attended the University of Minnesota at Duluth on a hockey scholarship. He was named the Western Colle-

giate Hockey Association's Freshman of the Year one season and an All-America the following season.

In May 1986, Brett signed a contract with the Calgary Flames, and played his first NHL game—in the Stanley Cup finals! The Flames lost to the Montreal Canadiens, yet Brett's dream of playing in the NHL, which had seemed impossible a few years earlier, had come true!

But it wasn't going to remain that simple. The following autumn, Brett had the worst day of his life. It started in Boston, Massachusetts, and ended up in Moncton, New Brunswick, Canada—one of the last places in the world that Brett wanted to be!

I came out of college highly rated as a goal-scorer. In my last season at the University of Minnesota, I had 52 goals and 84 points in 42 games. People said I had the hardest shot in college hockey.

In May, I left school to sign with the Flames. There was a lot of press attention, partly, I guess, because of who my dad is. I thought I had answered a lot of questions about following in his footsteps with my performance. I had even played two games in the Stanley Cup finals!

So by September, I went into training camp feeling pretty good. When I was growing up, my dad was a big star, and I dreamed of playing in the NHL. Now, here I was!

I thought I was doing great all during the preseason too. I scored seven

goals in seven exhibition games. Players rarely score a goal per game in the NHL, so I was proud of myself.

Then I had my worst day. It was the day before the regular season was to begin, and the team had flown to Boston to play the Bruins. We practiced in the morning, just like we always did. Then Bob Johnson, the coach of the team, called me into the office.

He told me I was being sent to the Flames' minor league club in Moncton, New Brunswick, in Canada! I had never heard of Moncton, never mind having no interest in playing hockey there! It was quite a blow to my ego. I don't think I've ever been more disappointed in my life.

Coach Johnson said, "You're a tremendous player and I know you have worked really hard. You'll be back with the team soon." But that didn't make me feel any better; it just made me angry. In fact, I think that was the worst thing the coach could have said: Telling me that I played well and worked hard but that they still didn't want me!

That made me think the situation was completely out of my control. It didn't matter that I had worked hard and played well. Calgary was an excellent team, and there were a lot of fine, experienced players ahead of me. I think the coach and the other team officials figured I would get more playing time with the minor league team in Moncton than if I stayed with Calgary. By playing more, they believed, I'd improve much faster than if I stayed and sat on the bench.

one of that made any difference to me. I was too angry to care about their reasons for sending me to Moncton. "How can they do this to me?" I asked myself. I felt that being sent down was the worst humiliation for a player. A lot of hockey players spend some time in the minor leagues when they first start out, but not, I thought,

players like me! I had shown that I could put the puck into the net. What else did they want?

I got really mad—at everybody. But I was scared, too. Coach Johnson had told me I was being sent down that very morning, and by the afternoon, I was on a plane to Moncton! I had no idea what I was facing. I was going somewhere I'd never been, where I *didn't* know anybody. And I didn't want to be going there!

I didn't even have my belongings with me, besides the clothes I'd brought for the trip to Boston. I arrived at the Moncton airport that

night and took a cab to the hotel I'd been told to go to. Then, the next morning, I had to go to practice without knowing a soul. It was weird.

But I got over the fear fairly quickly. I made some friends and rented a house with some teammates. Still, it was hard to get settled, and I wasn't sure I wanted to. Life in the minor leagues is different from life in the NHL. You live a lot more simply, you travel by bus a lot, and you play in many small cities and towns that you've never heard of. It wasn't that I had gotten used to the big-league life, but I had grown up watching my dad play in the NHL. I really wanted to be playing in famous places like Chicago Stadium and the Montreal Forum, not in Utica, New York; Hershey, Pennsylvania; and Moncton!

n the ice, it took me a while to adjust, too. I wasn't the only player who really wanted to make it to the NHL, and that made the competition sort of nasty. When you're in the minors, though, pretty soon you figure out that until you do well, you aren't going anywhere. So I decided

PLAYING FOR A MINOR LEAGUE TEAM WASN'T NEARLY AS GLAMOROUS AS PLAYING IN THE NHL.

I GREW UP WATCHING MY DAD PLAYING IN THE SPOTLIGHT-- AND I'M NOWHERE.

BRETT SOON DISCOVERED THAT HE WAS UP AGAINST SOME TOUGH COMPETITION TO GET BACK TO THE NHL. HE DECIDED TO WORK HARD ON HIS GAME-- AND WAIT FOR HIS CHANCE.

THIS IS THE SECOND TIME IN THE HISTORY OF THE AMERICAN HOCKEY LEAGUE THAT A PLAYER HAS SCORED 50 GOALS IN ONE SEASON.

to put the disappointment and anger aside. I started to bear down on myself and work hard on my game.

I always had been able to score goals. When you can do something that easily, you tend to keep doing it and little else. I realized that there were other aspects of the game I had to improve, like my skating ability and my defense.

I started the season off slowly and scored only eight goals in my first 28 games. But then I finally relaxed and started enjoying myself. I ended up having a great season. I scored 42 goals in the team's last 39 games and became the second rookie in the history of the American Hockey League to score 50 goals in one season!

When the season in Moncton was over, I joined Calgary for the play-offs. In four games, I had two goals and an assist. We lost to the Winnipeg Jets in the second round, but I went home figuring I would be in Calgary the following season. When Terry Crisp, who had been my coach in Moncton, became the Calgary coach during the spring, I thought I was set.

THE FOLLOWING SEASON BRETT WAS BACK WITH THE FLAMES.

BRETT'S DOING GREAT-- 26 GOALS AND 24 ASSISTS IN 52 GAMES. TOO BAD WE CAN'T GIVE HIM MORE PLAYING TIME.

BRETT WAS TRADED TO THE ST. LOUIS BLUES, BUT THIS TIME HE WAS HAPPY TO LEAVE THE FLAMES. THE BLUES WEREN'T A STRONG TEAM AND BRETT KNEW HE WOULD GET TO PLAY A LOT.

AND STARTING FOR THE BLUES, BRETT HULL...

I did make the team for the 1987-88 season, but I didn't get to play as much as I would have liked. I scored 26 goals and made 24 assists in 52 games, when, on March 7, 1988, I was traded to the St. Louis Blues.

This time I was delighted to be leaving the team! The Flames still had too many good players, and I was tired of fighting to get ice time. The Blues, on the other hand, weren't so good. I knew I would get to play a lot—and this time it would be in the NHL!

That day I was sent down to the minors really opened my eyes to some things. Coming out of college, I thought I had it made. But on my worst day, that changed suddenly. I couldn't be a star; I wasn't even in the NHL! I was completely humiliated. I had never had to deal with anything like that. It taught me that things are not always going to go your way, and that you have to be ready to handle them when they don't.

That experience made me realize that you have to look out for number 1—yourself!—because in the end, you are on your own. Maybe because I had a famous dad and because I could score goals, people had looked out for me during the previous few years. Maybe I began to think they would look out for me after I became a professional too. But that isn't the way life is. At some point, you have to start taking care of yourself. It's part of growing up.

My worst day taught me that I was going to have to bear down on myself and work harder. It probably took me a few more years to really take that lesson to heart. But when it finally got through, it made a big difference in my career.

I've always cared about hockey and about the way I played it—even when people thought I was too easygoing. But I have a different attitude toward the game now. I've learned how important it is to work hard, and I want to do the things that make me known as a team leader. I'm smarter now than I was before my worst day.

CHAPTER 3

DAN JANSEN

The speed skater had his sights on Olympic gold, until he fell—twice

 *an Jansen has been ranked among the best speed skaters in the world since 1984, when he finished fourth in the 500-meter race at the Winter Olympics in Sarajevo, Yugoslavia.*

In 1986, he won both the 500-meter and the 1,000-meter events of the World Cup, which is a five-month series of races. In 1988, he won the World Sprint Championships, which were held in his hometown of West Allis, Wisconsin. The championships are the biggest meet of the year. He has been among the Top 5 in the world at 500 and 1,000 meters every year since.

Dan was the youngest of nine children. All his brothers and sisters skated as kids, but only Dan

and his brother Mike stayed with skating until they had become world-class competitors. When he isn't skating, Dan works as a marketing representative for a Milwaukee company, studies marketing at the University of Wisconsin at Milwaukee, and plays golf. He got married in April 1990.

Dan's worst day occurred on February 14, 1988, when he was competing at the Winter Olympic Games in Calgary, Alberta, Canada. Dan, then age 22, was expected

to win medals in the 500-meter and 1,000-meter events. His first race, the 500, was on February 14. Here's what happened.

I had been skating well all week in practice, feeling the best I had ever felt. When I stepped off the ice the day before the 500-meter race, I just knew I could win the gold medal.

I was staying at the Olympic Village, and about 6 o'clock on the morning of the race, one of my teammates woke me to say that I had a telephone call. It was my mother. She was calling from the hospital back home in West Allis, where my 27-year-old sister, Jane, was being treated for leukemia. Leukemia is a form of cancer that affects the blood.

Jane had been very sick for more than a year. I knew when I went to Calgary for the Olympics that her condition was getting worse, but our family all agreed that I should go on and skate. Skating was my life. Jane knew that; she had been a skater, too. When she first started getting sick, she told us all that we had to go ahead and live our lives. She didn't want us to deprive ourselves of anything because of her illness.

My mother called that morning to tell me that Jane's condition had grown much worse and that her doctors did not think she would live through the day. Jane was on a respirator, which is a machine that helps very sick people breathe, and couldn't speak. But one of my brothers, Mike, who was also at the hospital, held the phone to Jane's ear so I could talk to her for what would probably be the last time.

After I got off the phone, my brother Jim, who was in Calgary to see me race, and I talked for a couple of hours. Jim is 11 years older than me, and it helped me by talking with him. I had asked my mom whether she thought I should go ahead and race that night. She had said yes, but I kept wondering how I could skate if Jane died before my race.

I was hoping that Jane didn't die before the race, and I told Jim that I had heard that people could live for weeks when they were hooked up to respirators. But Jim gave it to me straight. "She's not going to be around for your race," he said. He thought I had better start preparing for that fact. After a while, Jim left and I tried to eat some breakfast.

Then, around 10 o'clock, Jim called to tell me that Jane had died. When I got off the phone, I went up to my room, lay on the bed, and cried for an hour. I kept thinking about whether I should skate that night. I wasn't sure my mom was right to say that I should, and I didn't really feel like skating, but the more I thought about it, the more I realized that Jane would have wanted me to skate. I decided that I would try to win the race for Jane.

The day passed slowly. I tried to eat lunch, and to loosen up, I went jogging with a teammate. Finally, it was time to leave for the speed-skating oval. We had a team meeting. The other U.S. skaters said they would all dedicate their performances to Jane. That made me feel good.

There was a huge crowd at the oval, and lots of people were cheering and waving banners when I went out to warm up before my race. Right away, I noticed that my skates didn't feel the way they had the day before in practice. I was slipping on the ice. I had been thinking about Jane all day instead of preparing myself mentally for the race. I told myself that when the race started, I would simply put myself on automatic and go skate.

My first start was a false start. When the starter fired his gun again, the race began, and I knew immediately that I must be doing something wrong. In the first 100 meters of a speed-skating race, you have to be quick and powerful, but my skates were slipping out to the sides as I was pushing. I wasn't getting 100 percent power.

he skating oval is 400 meters. In the 500, we skate once around the oval and then down the straightaway to the finish line. I never made it that far. Two steps into the first turn, my left skate slipped right out from under me, and I fell. A 500 meter race takes about 37 seconds, so there is no way a skater can get back into a race after he falls. That was the end of my dream of winning the gold medal in the 500. I was numb with disbelief. I thought, "What else can happen to me today?"

The 1,000-meter race was four days later. My family decided not to have Jane's funeral until after that race. My sister Janet, my brother Mike, and his wife all came to Calgary to be with me.

During the warm-ups the night of the 1,000-meter race, I felt better than I had before the 500 meters, and I got a good start. I was on pace to set a world record—until just 200 meters from the finish line, I fell! Again, I couldn't believe it.

I was really disappointed. I had spent the last four years training for the Olympics and I hadn't even finished one race. But I was also

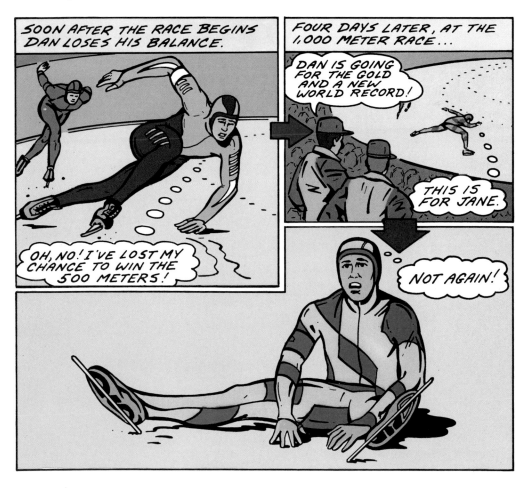

relieved that it was over. Now I could go home and be with my family. That night we flew home to Wisconsin for Jane's funeral.

Although my Olympic hopes had ended for the time being, I didn't give up skating. I needed to stay busy. I didn't want to sit home and feel sorry for myself. A week later I was back in Calgary to receive the Olympic Spirit Award from the U.S. Olympic Committee. After that, I went home to be with my family for a few days. Then I went back on the World Cup speed skating circuit. And I skated well. I ended up winning the 1988 World Cup season title in the 1,000 meters and finishing second in the 500.

I've discovered that I changed a lot because of my worst day. When I accepted the Olympic Spirit Award, I said that even though the Calgary Olympics had not gone the way I had planned, I gained a lot from it. I had met many people and made a lot of friends. And I had learned some lessons: I learned that things don't always go the way you

AFTER THE OLYMPICS ARE OVER, DAN GOES HOME TO BE WITH HIS FAMILY.

I MISS JANE. LOSING HER MAKES ME REALIZE WHAT'S REALLY IMPORTANT IN LIFE.

DAN IS SKATING WELL AGAIN. HE KNOWS THAT IF HE LOSES, IT'S NOT THE END OF THE WORLD -- AS LONG AS HE TRIES HIS BEST.

planned and that not everyone can be a winner.

efore the day Jane died, my absolute top priority had always been to win. If I had a bad day in practice, I would be upset. Winning speed-skating races was more important than just about anything. Now I enjoy the skating itself more. I am still intense during practice and races and I still try to do my best to win, but if I don't do well, I know it's not the end of the world. I tell myself that I will do better the next time. I don't know if I'm a better skater because of this attitude, but I think I'm a better and happier person.

Right now, I'm training for the 1992 Olympics, which will be held in Albertville, France. If I make the team again and get to go to the Games, I will skate the best I can. But if I don't win, I won't be disappointed—as long as I have done my best.

I have learned that there are more important things in life than gold medals.

CHAPTER 4

EARVIN (MAGIC) JOHNSON, JR.

Injured for the first time in his life, Magic felt lost without his teammates

he Los Angeles Lakers' great guard, Earvin "Magic" Johnson, has a big, broad smile, the kind that cheers you up immediately. Ask him what his worst day was, and he flashes that smile and says "I don't have worst days."

He has not had many, that's for sure. From 1977 to 1980, Magic played on teams that won championships on three levels: high school, college, and professional. In the past decade, he has led the Lakers to four more National Basketball Association championships and seven Western Conference titles!

Magic was born in Lansing, Michigan, in 1959, one of 10 children. He has always loved playing basketball, and would get up at dawn to practice dribbling on the street outside his

house. At Everett High School, he averaged nearly 25 points a game over three years, led the team to the state title his senior year, and earned the nickname Magic.

As a sophomore at Michigan State University in 1979, Magic led the Spartans to the National Collegiate Athletics Association (NCAA) championship. That spring, the Lakers selected Magic as the number 1 pick in the NBA draft.

In 1979-80, he led the Lakers to the NBA title and became the first

rookie in league history to be named the Most Valuable Player of a championship series. Although he usually played guard, the 20-year-old Magic started at center, replacing the great Kareem Abdul-Jabbar, who was injured, in the final game of the series. He scored 42 points, grabbed 15 rebounds, and handed out seven assists!

Since then, Magic has won three regular-season MVP awards, two more play-off MVP awards, and one All-Star Game MVP trophy. A 10-time All-Star, he has led the league in steals twice and in assists four times. Entering the 1990-91 season, he has averaged 11 assists, seven re-bounds and nearly 20 points per game over his 12 years in the NBA. No, there have not been many bad days in Magic's career.

But, Magic says, there was one day—only five months after his amazing performance in the 1980 championship finals, when he was still feeling on top of the world—that brought him crashing down to earth with a loud thud. That day was November 18, 1980. And, for a man who never has any worst days, Magic says, this day was pretty bad.

ll I did on my worst day was try to change direction. It began early in the second quarter of a game against the Kansas City Kings (now the Sacramento Kings), and I was guarding Hawkeye Whitney. I went to make a cut and I felt something pop in my left knee.

he previous week against the Atlanta Hawks, Tom Burleson had fallen on the knee and had hurt it a little. Then in a game against Dallas, Tom LeGarde fell on it, so I guess the knee must have been a little strained already. But this time there was no contact with anybody or anything. I cut and it was as if the knee said, "Magic, I'm not going with you." The cartilage, which is the connective tissue where bones join, tore.

I knew right away that it was serious because I tried to keep walking and couldn't. It also hurt a lot. Something was very wrong. A lot of things go through your mind when something like that happens to you. I had never been hurt in my life. I didn't know how to deal with the pain or with the condition of being hurt. Immediately, I wondered if my basketball career was over.

The doctor said he could fix my knee with an operation but that it was going to take time to get the knee back in shape. After the doctor operated, he put my leg in a cast. Then he prescribed some exercises to strengthen the knee. "You are going to have to work as hard as you have ever worked in your life," he said to me.

Mentally, I really had to regroup and then dedicate myself completely to coming back. The first time I stood up and put pressure on the knee, it hurt me so much that I could barely stand it. Even when I tried to lift some light weights, it hurt—a lot! For months I was in pain. When you are injured, you have to learn to tolerate it.

The physical pain was bad, but that wasn't even the worst part. The worst thing is that you are by yourself. Being hurt is the loneliest feeling in the world. You have to do everything yourself. No one else can make your knee better. You are the only one who can do it—by working through the pain and building all the muscles and everything back up.

eanwhile, you aren't out there doing what you love to do, playing basketball and being a part of the team. Now you have to have therapy and work out on the knee twice a day. You aren't working out with your teammates anymore; you feel like an outsider. Even when you're in the clubhouse, you are outside the group. The jive is going around, the talking and the conversation. But you are not a part of it

FIVE MONTHS AFTER BEING NAMED THE NBA FINALS MVP AS A ROOKIE, MAGIC JOHNSON WAS FEELING ON TOP OF THE WORLD. THEN A KNEE INJURY SENT HIM CRASHING DOWN TO EARTH.

POP!

YOU ARE GOING TO HAVE TO WORK AS HARD AS YOU HAVE EVER WORKED TO MAKE YOUR KNEE STRONG ENOUGH FOR BASKETBALL AGAIN.

because you are not a part of the team. You have to deal with that. It's a very lonely feeling.

fter the cast was taken off, I did a week of intensive therapy at the National Athletic Health Institute in Los Angeles, California. After that week, I felt as if I knew how a factory worker feels. All I heard was the weights I was working with to strengthen my knee. Clang! Back down. Clang! Back up. You sit there and say "Maaaaan!" Clang! That noise is all you hear. It was tough.

Finally, I went home to Michigan for a few weeks. I spent some time with my family—I'm very close to them—and I worked out at Jenison Field House at Michigan State University. My friend, Dr. Charles Tucker, supervised my conditioning.

It was such a long road to getting back in shape that sometimes it seemed as if I would never be ready. When I was first working with Charles, I would just show up when I was supposed to and work out. But as the knee got stronger and the time for me to rejoin the team got closer, I

I DON'T FEEL LIKE I'M PART OF THE TEAM ANYMORE.

OKAY. NOW LET'S TRY DOING 50 REPS.

MAAAAAN! THIS IS HARD!

MAGIC VISITED HIS FAMILY IN MICHIGAN DURING THE LAST WEEKS OF HIS RECOVERY. HE CONTINUED TO WORK HARD TO MAKE HIS KNEE STRONGER. THE MORE IMPROVEMENT MAGIC SAW, THE MORE EXCITED HE BECAME.

HEY, CHARLES. I CAN FINALLY FEEL A DIFFERENCE.

began to get excited again. Now, by the time Charles showed up, I'd already be at the field house, warming up. I did all kinds of work to get ready to play again: lifted weights, ran miles, did wind sprints and jumping drills.

t last, I was ready to join the Lakers again. They were on the road. I scrimmaged some with them and finally got to take off the heavy brace that I had been wearing to protect my knee. That was a relief!

By then I was eager to begin playing again. But I was also really nervous. I wondered if the knee was going to hold up. That's the kind of thing that goes through your mind. I was excited and anxious at the same time. You just don't know for sure until you take that first big cut on the court in a game. That tells you a lot. When the knee does hold up, you say, "Wow, this may work out after all." Then a smile comes to your face and a lot of uncertainties go out of your mind. You become more aggressive on the court.

I had missed 45 games—three

OKAY, EARVIN. LET'S TEST THAT KNEE IN A SCRIMMAGE.

I HOPE IT HOLDS UP.

MAGIC HAD BEEN OUT THREE MONTHS BY THE TIME HE PLAYED HIS FIRST GAME AFTER THE INJURY. HE HAD WORKED HARD TO MAKE IT BACK. AND IT FELT GREAT!

months!—by the time I played my first game since the injury. It was against the New Jersey Nets. The Forum, where we play our home games, was sold out. I scored 12 points in 24 minutes. That's well below my average, but considering everything that I had been through, it was just fine. I was back!

y injury taught me a few things. I realized that the members of your family are the ones whom you lean on when you are hurt. They are the ones who really understand. Your teammates are wrapped up in playing—just like you would be if you were playing—and they can't fully understand what you are going through. But your family loves you no matter what happens. When I was hurt, I needed them even more. And they were there for me.

The other important thing that I learned from my worst day is that as quickly as you can rise to the top of the world, you can fall just as fast. I'd had such success—in high school, in college, and then in my first year in the NBA—that it was a real shock to be hurt and out of action. I guess that I had taken it for granted that I had been healthy and able to play basketball. I never thought in my mind that I could get hurt. But, wham! It just happened.

After that, you thank God every night, every practice, every day, that you are able to play, able to perform —even that you're just able to walk.

CHAPTER 5

SHAUN JORDAN

A loose draw-string left this swimmer up the pool without a swimsuit

hen swimmer Shaun Jordan arrived at the University of Texas, in Austin, in August 1986, he was six feet tall but weighed only 139 pounds. He was so skinny that his teammates nicknamed him Scrawn, and the coach didn't let him swim for the team for a year. Less than two years later, Shaun was awarded a gold medal at the Summer Olympics in Seoul, South Korea!

Shaun had placed sixth at the trails in the 100-meter freestyle. He made the U.S. Olympic team and went to Seoul as an alternate. In the Olympics, alternates often swim in the early rounds of the relay competition so that the top swimmers, who race in many events, can rest. Shaun replaced seven-medal winner Matt Biondi in the preliminary round of the 400-meter freestyle relay, and his fine performance helped the U.S. team earn the best lane placement in the final. When the U.S. relay team won that race, Shaun got a gold medal! Shaun is expected to be a member of the U.S. Olympic team in 1992.

In four years of swimming for the University of Texas, Shaun helped the Longhorns win four straight National Collegiate Athletic Associa-

tion (NCAA) championships. He has won 15 NCAA titles, including the 1989 100-yard freestyle championship. Shaun also had 15 victories in the Southwest Conference championships from 1988 to 1991.

Shaun grew up in Dallas, Texas. He was not recruited by many college coaches, partly because of his size and partly because he did not take swimming seriously when he was in high school. He used to goof around and skip practice. In college, Shaun realized that he could be a great swimmer if he worked harder, and he has. But he still doesn't take things too seriously. That may explain why he can look back and laugh at the worst day he ever had.

It happened on December 4, 1987. Shaun was 19 years old and he was competing in only his second college swim meet, at Berkeley, California.

e were swimming against the University of California at Berkeley, which had one of the best teams in the country. Our team was young, and no one expected us to be any good.

Judging from the way the meet was going, those people were right. We were losing just about every race. My best event is the 50-meter freestyle, but I was beaten in that race. I lost again in the 100-meter freestyle.

As if the lopsided score was not bad enough, the weather that day was miserable! It was pouring rain, and it was windy and cold too. There was no locker room for visitors, so to keep warm between races, we huddled in the pool's pump room, which was a dark, damp room that reeked of chlorine.

inally, it was time for the last event of the day, the 400-yard freestyle relay. I was the anchor, which meant that I would be the last of the four Texas swimmers to swim 100 meters. We had already lost the meet, but my teammates and I were hoping to have at least one good race. As a freshman, I felt I had a lot to prove, so I was especially eager to do well.

When the race started, I was standing on the pool deck. I was cheering on the first two swimmers on my team, but mainly, I was trying to keep warm until my turn came. I had on six layers of clothes over my swimsuit! I was wearing gloves and socks and a parka that went below my knees. My plan was to strip off the clothes layer by layer until it was time to jump onto the starting blocks and dive in.

The California relay team was beating us easily. When our third swimmer dived in, he was about two body lengths behind his opponent. I started to strip down to my swimsuit when my teammate was about 20 yards from finishing his leg of the race. Just as he approached the wall, I jumped onto the block and put on my goggles. But I didn't notice the draw-string on my swimsuit was untied.

As soon as my teammate touched the wall, I dove into the water. *Whoa!* My suit slid right down to my knees! I couldn't stop, so as I swam, I tried to reach back with one hand and pull my suit up. But I couldn't. Then, even before I had gone the first 25 yards, the suit came off completely!

The public address announcer noticed my problem right away and said, jokingly, "Now swimming in the white suit for Texas...." I knew everyone was laughing and pointing at me. They could see that I was totally naked in the water.

At first, I felt sick. This was easily the most embarrassing thing that had ever happened to me. But I kept swimming. I figured if I quit the race, I *really* would have been ridiculed.

After a while, I began thinking that if I could just win the race, maybe I could save some face. Although my opponent had a big lead at the start, I started gaining on him. My adrenaline was really pumping and I was swimming fast. As we raced

WHAT A MISERABLE DAY FOR AN OUTDOOR SWIM MEET.

OKAY, THE 4x100 METER RELAY TEAM IS UP NEXT.

WE'RE SO FAR BEHIND. I'VE GOT TO TRY TO MAKE UP SOME TIME.

AS SHAUN DIVES IN...

down the final length of the pool, I caught up to him, but he touched the wall first at the finish.

I t didn't seem to matter who had won, though. Everybody at the meet was going wild. My teammates were doubled over with laughter, and even the California swimmers were cheering for me! I swam back to the middle of the pool, found my suit—it was just floating around out there—and put it on. When I stepped out of the pool, my coach was still laughing, but he patted me on the back and

said, "Way to keep swimming!"

That incident was embarrassing for me, but it turned out to be a great thing for the team. It took the sting out of our defeat. The score of the meet was California 79, Texas 34, one of the worst losses in the team's history. But we could laugh about it because of what happened to me. It really broke the tension and lightened the depressed feelings we had about having done so poorly.

I also realized that everyone does something silly or embarrassing at some point in his or her life. If people laugh at you then, you shouldn't feel

hurt. They aren't laughing because they think you're stupid; they are laughing because what has happened is *funny*. When something funny happens, people laugh! You have to be able to laugh at yourself, too. Try to step out of yourself and look through someone else's eyes at what you did. You'll probably start laughing, too! It's important to be able to do that.

Another good thing came out of that day. Because our team was beaten so badly, we worked harder during the rest of the season. We kept reminding ourselves of that day, and it motivated us to push ourselves more and more in practice.

In January, the California team came to Dallas to compete in a big invitational meet among six of the top teams in the country, and we beat them. In March, we won the NCAA championship, and we have been ranked Number 1 in the country ever since. During the summer of 1988, five of us qualified for the Olympic team!

Oh, yes, I learned another lesson from my worst day: Be sure that the drawstring on your suit is tied *before* you dive into the water!

CHAPTER 6

JACKIE JOYNER-KERSEE

Jackie's team expected to win the state title, then the lights went out

any people consider track and field star Jackie Joyner-Kersee to be the greatest female athlete in the world today. At the 1988 Olympics in Seoul, South Korea, Jackie was awarded two gold medals—one for winning the long jump, with an Olympic-record leap of 24' 3 1/4", and one for winning the heptathlon, with a world-record point total.

The heptathlon is a two-day, seven-event competition that requires an awesome combination of speed, strength, and jumping ability. The events are the 100-meter hurdles, shot put, high jump, 200-meter dash, long jump, javelin throw, and 800-meter run. Athletes score points based on the times of their runs, the heights or lengths of their jumps, and the distances of their throws. At the Olympics, Jackie scored 7,291 points,

the fifth time she had scored more than 7,000 points. Only one other woman has ever even topped 7,000!

No woman had ever been named the Man of the Year by The Sporting News, *a national weekly sports newspaper. Jackie was, in 1988. And very few have won the Sullivan Award, which is given by the Amateur Athletic Union each year to the best amateur athlete in the United States. Jackie won it in 1986. In col-

lege, at the University of California at Los Angeles (UCLA), Jackie also captained the women's basketball team and was named All-University Athlete of the Year three times.

But in many ways, it is amazing that Jackie ever made it to college at all. The second of four children, Jackie grew up in a poor family in a rough neighborhood in East St. Louis, Illinois. Sometimes, money was so tight that her family could not afford heating fuel. They'd sleep in the kitchen, next to the cooking stove, because it provided the only heat in the house. Other times, there was nothing to eat but mayonnaise sandwiches. "I didn't mind," Jackie says. "They were good!"

That positive attitude, and two strict parents who made sure she worked hard at school and stayed out of trouble, helped Jackie excel. She began competing in a local track program at age 9, and by high school, she was a star athlete—as well as a top student.

Today, Jackie lives in Los Angeles, but she still visits East St. Louis often. She has formed the JJK Community Foundation for raising money to help the children of her hometown. One of her goals is to raise enough money to reopen the community center where she first competed.

Although Jackie is best known today for her accomplishments in track and field, it was an experience in a high school basketball game that

Jackie remembers as the worst day she ever had. It happened on March 21, 1978. Jackie was 16 years old.

I was in the 10th grade at Lincoln High School in East St. Louis. Although I was only a freshman (Lincoln High went from 10th through 12th grades so we 10th-graders were considered "freshmen"), I was one of the starters and leading scorers on the girls' basketball team. We were a pretty young team. There were only two seniors on the squad, but we were talented and we did well.

On my worst day, we were in Edwardsville, Illinois, playing the girls' team from Centralia High in the semifinals of the state sectional championships. We were having a great season. We had won 19 of the 21 games we had played, and everyone expected us to go on to the state tournament. We were really excited to be playing in the sectionals. A lot of people from East St. Louis had come to Edwardsville with us to see the game. So, it was very important to all of us that we win.

When the game began, everything was clicking for us as a team. On defense, we pressed Centralia and that forced them to make a lot of turnovers. On offense, we passed well and took good shots. The Centralia girls didn't seem to be able to do much of anything, so we went ahead easily. We were leading by about 15 points late in the first half.

Then all of a sudden, the lights

42

went out! Literally! It was very strange, almost spooky, to be sitting in this gym with all these people and no lights. We ended up sitting around in the dark for an hour.

uring that hour, my teammates and I tried to relax. We didn't discuss the game at all. I think we were more concerned with why the lights had gone out and whether or not they were going to come back on. We had such a big lead that we were confident we were going to win the game.

There really wasn't any reason to talk about it, or so we thought.

But after the lights finally came back on, it was clear that the Centralia girls had not been sitting around during the blackout. They came back onto the court and started playing like a team. They must have discussed the game and figured out what they needed to do.

While we had been relaxing, Centralia had been stretching to keep warm and talking about strategy. They had regrouped. And they were really fired up.

We, on the other hand, couldn't do

THE LINCOLN HIGH BASKETBALL TEAM WAS FAVORED TO BEAT CENTRALIA HIGH IN THE SECTIONAL BASKETBALL CHAMPIONSHIP. LINCOLN HIGH HAD A BIG LEAD IN THE FIRST HALF WHEN...

... SUDDENLY, THE LIGHTS WENT OUT.

anything right. We were cold and stiff because we hadn't done anything to keep ourselves warmed up and loose during the long delay. And we couldn't connect on our passes or shots because we just weren't into the game anymore. Once we saw that the momentum had shifted, it got even worse. Everyone panicked and began playing individual ball. Instead of making passes and setting picks to work plays as a team, we each tried to win the game by ourselves.

I was as bad as everyone else, dribbling toward the basket and putting up poor shots instead of passing to an open teammate. I had been one of the leading scorers all year, so I guess I thought I should just try harder to score some baskets on my own.

It didn't work. When we stopped playing as a team, we just fell apart. And the worst thing was, we didn't know how to deal with that. Instead of settling down and working ourselves back into the game, we started getting angry at the referees for every call that went against us.

Slowly, Centralia began to catch up. They took the lead late in the

WHILE THE LIGHTS WERE OUT, CENTRALIA HIGH USED THE DELAY TO REGROUP.

I CAN WIN THE GAME FOR US.

WE'VE TOTALLY FALLEN APART. I'VE GOT TO TRY TO SAVE THE GAME.

OVER HERE, JACKIE!

SHE SHOULD PASS TO ME. I'M THE ONE WHO'S OPEN.

game, but we held on to force over-time. We still weren't playing as a team, though, and in the end, Centralia won the game, 48-47.

We were stunned. We couldn't believe that our great season was over so suddenly. We were supposed to be going to the state championship, and here we were, on a bus, going home to East St. Louis—as losers!

Our team spent the rest of the year trying to get over that game. We watched the game tapes over and over. We could see that we were in a good groove at the beginning. We had warmed up well, we were perspiring, and we were playing the way we ought to before the lights went out.

e saw that after the delay we weren't perspiring anymore. We were really cold and disorganized. When we watched the tape, we felt again that horrible feeling of disappointment that we had felt after the game.

Finally, we understood what had happened: We had gotten bigheaded. We thought that because we

WHAT HAPPENED OUT THERE? YOU WERE SUPPOSED TO PLAY LIKE A TEAM.

LOOK AT US. WE WEREN'T EVEN WARMED UP WHEN WE CAME BACK ON THE COURT.

WHAT MADE ME THINK I COULD MAKE THAT SHOT?

WE WERE BIGHEADED AND TOOK OUR LEAD FOR GRANTED.

THE MEMORY OF THAT LOSS TO CENTRALIA MADE JACKIE AND HER TEAM-MATES WORK HARDER THAN EVER. IN JACKIE'S SENIOR YEAR, LINCOLN HIGH WON THE STATE CHAMPIONSHIP.

were up by 15 points, the other team was going to lay down and hand us the game.

For me, it was a great lesson about teamwork. I realized that if one team member lets up in a sport like basketball, that attitude spreads like a contagious disease. And then you need to have one person start doing something special to get things turned back around. If that team member starts working really hard on defense—because you can always play good defense—it can spark the whole team. The other players say "Uh-oh, so-and-so is doing good. I'd better go all out, too." But if every member of the team is out to lunch, as we were against Centralia, you're in trouble.

In the long run, that game helped our team because we were able to keep that feeling of disappointment and anger at ourselves for messing up in the back of our minds. We were determined not to go through that again. So we worked hard to do better, and we did better. The next year we made it to the state championship finals, and in my senior year we won the Illinois State championship!

My worst day taught me a lot about leadership. I thought about what I had done that night—I had been one of the leading scorers with 10 points and 9 rebounds—and what I could have done as one of the team leaders.

First of all, while the lights were out, I should have helped us keep our minds on the game. Not once during that blackout did any of us say "Hey, this is only the first half of the game. There's still a lot of basketball to play." If we had kept focused on the game a little more, we might have won.

But then I was only a freshman. The next year I was more experienced and more mature. I took it upon myself to make sure that we kept our minds more on our business. Sometimes, my teammates would get mad at me or tease me because I confronted them or told the coach if I thought someone was doing something that could stop the team from succeeding, like hanging out with a boyfriend instead of going to practice.

That didn't make me too popular at first, but after a while, my teammates respected me for doing it. They knew that it would help us become champions.

I also learned that it takes more than talent to become a champion. That season, before my worst day, we had gotten away with a lot because we were talented. But the experience in the Centralia game taught me that talent is not enough. You have to be totally dedicated to your sport and to what you are trying to accomplish.

I learned to ask myself whether I was doing the things that were in my best interest as an athlete and in the best interest of the team. And I learned that as a leader, I had to be willing to make the same demands of my teammates. I feel that if you are on a team and you let a teammate get away with doing something that isn't in the best interest of the team, you are as much to blame as the person doing it.

or example, once during a track practice, we were running a long route around the neighborhood. We stopped off for a snack at a friend's house and then took a short-cut back to school so the coach wouldn't know we hadn't run the full course. Later, I felt so bad that I went out and ran the course in the dark! I knew that running the full course was the right thing to do.

In a team sport, you have to be ready to do your job, but every single member of the team has to be ready to do her job, too. It takes an entire team to win a game; one person can't do it alone. After the Centralia game, I made sure that we had a lot of team meetings to talk about each person's role. We went over who was supposed to be setting picks and who was supposed to get the rebounds and who was supposed to concentrate on defense. The people who score the points are the ones who get their names into the newspapers, but they couldn't score if everyone else didn't do her job, too.

That lesson about teamwork is also important in track and field, even though it is more of an individual sport than basketball. In track, you are still a part of a team, and you still have to do your job by doing your best in your events. And all the other members of the team have to do *their* job to win the team title. That's especially important when you are on a relay team. You can be the fastest runner around, but if the three other members of the relay team don't get you the baton in good position, you can't win.

y worst day also taught me that you can never relax. It's hard to keep up your intensity for an entire basketball game, but you must. And keeping up your intensity during a track meet can be even harder, especially when you compete in the kinds of events in which I compete.

The heptathlon events are spread over two days. I have to stay ready to compete, both physically and mentally. I know that I had better not get too relaxed between events. If I do I might not perform up to my ability— and I might lose!

I enjoy talking to competitors and other people at a meet, but I always make sure that I'm stretching or doing whatever it is I should be doing to get ready for my competition. And if the conversation starts getting too far off the subject of what our purpose is, I'll excuse myself and go off and concentrate on getting ready to compete.

So there are a lot of things I learned from my worst day. Most of all, though, I think that the Centralia game taught me that you can't take winning for granted. If you do, you will relax too much and you might lose. And you should *never* underestimate your opponent. To this day, I don't ever underestimate my competition. No matter how good everyone says I am or how many times I have beaten someone or how many world records I have, I know that that other person might beat me if I don't do my best.

I don't ever again want to know that feeling I had the day the lights went out!

CHAPTER 7

JULIE KRONE

When her mom became ill, the jockey found herself on a bumpy track—all alone

Julie Krone, the most successful female jockey in history, was practically born to the sport of horse racing. Raised on a farm in Michigan, she was introduced to horses by her mother, Judi, who trained them for shows. At the age of 3, Julie began taking rides alone on her pony, Daisy. When she was 5, she won a blue ribbon at the Berrien County Youth Fair horse show—in the 21-and-under division!

Julie saw her first horse race, at Detroit Race Course, when she was 8. Her parents separated when she was a teenager, and when she was 15, her mom took her to Churchill Downs, in Louisville, Kentucky, where she got a job exercising horses. That summer, she started riding professionally, competing in minor races on tracks at Michigan county fairs.

In 1980, Julie went to Florida to live with her grandparents and to give riding a serious shot. Within weeks, she had her first mount, or ride, at a major track. It was a horse named Tiny Star in the third race at Tampa Bay Downs Race Track. Tiny Star finished second! On February 12, Julie rode her first winner, a horse named Lord Farckle, also at Tampa Bay.

After a long struggle to get good opportunities in a sport that is dominated by men, Julie came into her own in 1987. That year she became the first woman to win riding titles at a major racetrack: at Monmouth Park and then at the Meadowlands, both in New Jersey. In August of that year, Julie enjoyed the best day of her career when she rode six winners—a feat no other female jockey had ever accomplished.

Since then, the 4'10½", 100-pound jockey has set all kinds of records for female riders. She has won more money and ridden more winners than any other woman, and she became the first woman to ride in the prestigious Breeders' Cup in 1988. She has also come back following a number of injuries from falls off speeding racehorses.

"I don't think of her as a girl jockey anymore," says fellow jockey Richard Migliore. Indeed, Julie has become one of the best jockeys—male or female—in the United States.

For Julie, all her success in the summer of 1987 was tied in a strange way to the worst day she ever had. That day occurred nearly a year and a half earlier, in May 1986, when Julie was 23.

I was living in New Jersey, because I was riding at Garden State Park in Cherry Hill at the time. My mom had moved from Michigan to Bushnell, Florida. She had been having health problems, and I knew she planned to see the doctor. I didn't know if her condition was serious.

The telephone rang, and it was Mom, calling me from the hospital in Leesburg, near Bushnell. "I have something to tell you," she said, "and it's really bad news." She was obviously very upset, and she was crying. She said that her doctor had told her to get "her affairs" organized, because she was probably going to die soon.

The doctors had discovered that she had cancer, and it had already spread through much of her body. The doctors said it was very serious and that even if they tried to treat it, they didn't think she could live for more than a year or two.

I remember I was sitting in my room, crying and thinking all the things you think about at a time like that: how unfair it is, all the things I should have done for her, how much I loved her. My mother and I have always been very close. She's the one who introduced me to horses, and she has always encouraged me to follow my dreams. Even when other people thought I could never be a professional jockey, she was behind me.

I didn't know what to say to my mom. You feel so helpless at a time like that. There's not really anything you can say except that you'll be there for them. Other than that you feel pretty stupid, because nothing you say is going to fix the person's cancer.

There was nothing I could do, so I went ahead to the track. I did terribly that day. I got left in the gate in one race, I fell off a horse pulling up after another race, and I dropped my whip in a third.

ntil that day, I'd been having a pretty good meeting, which is what a racing season at a particular track is called. A fair number of the horses I had ridden had won races. But after my mother told me about her illness, I started riding horribly.

Everything I did was wrong. All I could think about was my mom being sick. I kept doing dumb things at the track.

When you are assigned to ride a horse, you have to report to the jockey's room ahead of the race's starting time. I would leave home on time, but because I was so involved thinking about my mom, or so tired from not sleeping the night before, I'd end up arriving late and being taken off the horse—and he'd win the race! Or another horse would beat my mount by a nose, because I had dropped my whip and couldn't

JULIE KRONE WAS HAVING A GOOD MEETING IN THE SPRING OF 1986.

GREAT WIN, JULIE. YOU'VE REALLY BEEN RIDING WELL.

YEP. AND I OWE IT ALL TO MY MOM. SHE PUT ME ON A HORSE WHEN I WAS THREE YEARS OLD AND I'VE BEEN THERE EVER SINCE!

THEN ONE DAY, JULIE'S MOM CALLED FROM THE HOSPITAL. MRS. KRONE HAD CANCER, AND THE DOCTORS THOUGHT SHE DIDN'T HAVE LONG TO LIVE.

I LOVE YOU, MOM. I WISH THERE WAS SOMETHING I COULD DO!

whip my horse to urge him home.

It seemed like day after day terrible things were happening. Sometimes I realized that not concentrating on what I was doing was pretty dangerous. Then I'd tell myself, I'd better pay attention here, or maybe I shouldn't be riding. But I needed the money, so I had to ride. I felt helpless.

Meanwhile, my mother was having a horrible time. The cancer had spread all over her internal organs; it was on her liver, gall bladder, intestines, pancreas—virtually everywhere from the bottom of her heart to the female reproductive organs.

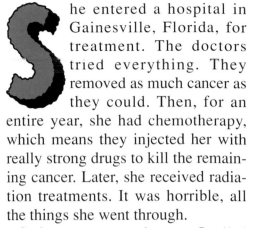

She entered a hospital in Gainesville, Florida, for treatment. The doctors tried everything. They removed as much cancer as they could. Then, for an entire year, she had chemotherapy, which means they injected her with really strong drugs to kill the remaining cancer. Later, she received radiation treatments. It was horrible, all the things she went through.

So it was strange whenever I called her up. She would ask, "How'd you

LATER THAT DAY...

SOMETHING MUST BE BOTHERING JULIE. SHE'S NOT RIDING AS WELL AS SHE HAD BEEN.

WHILE HER MOTHER WENT THROUGH PAINFUL TREATMENTS FOR HER CANCER, JULIE CONTINUED TO RACE POORLY. HER MOM KNEW SOMETHING WAS WRONG, BUT JULIE WAS RELUCTANT TO TALK ABOUT IT.

MOM, HOW CAN I TELL YOU ABOUT MY PROBLEMS? YOU'RE FIGHTING FOR YOUR LIFE!

I'M YOUR MOTHER AND IT HELPS ME TO THINK THAT I CAN STILL HELP YOU. WIN ONE FOR ME, OKAY?

THAT'S IT! I'M GOING TO GO OUT AND WIN SOME RACES FOR MY MOM.

do today?" and I would answer, "Oh, fine." Next she would ask, "How many did you win?" and I would be thinking, "How can I tell her my riding problems when she's fighting for her life?" I just couldn't talk about it.

This went on for months. As usual, I continued riding at the different racetracks when they were open. Garden State closed in June, and I started riding, poorly, at Monmouth Park. Eventually, my mother noticed that I wasn't talking to her about how things were going at the track, the way I usually did. "You never call me and tell me about your problems," she said.

"Mom, how am I going to tell you about my problems?" I said to her. "You're fighting for your life!"

She said, "But I'm your mother. I have to help you with those things." I didn't know that she really *did* want to hear about my problems. I guess that's a mother's instinct no matter what condition she's in. Later, my mother said that giving me support really helped her. So much of the time she felt so sick that she just wanted to roll up into a little ball and

THE NEXT YEAR, JULIE WAS ON A WINNING STREAK AT MONMOUTH RACE TRACK.

THAT LAST WIN PUT YOU IN THE LEAD.

CALL MY MOM. I WANT HER HERE WHEN I WIN THE MEETING TITLE.

JULIE AND HER MOM WERE BOTH WINNERS THAT YEAR. JULIE WON A SECOND MEETING AT THE MEADOWLANDS, AND HER MOM BEAT THE CANCER.

stay in her bed. But knowing that I needed her encouraged Mom to make an effort to do things.

So I began telling her all the good things and all the bad things again. Mostly, it was bad. I was still having trouble concentrating on my riding because I was so worried about her. One day while she was taking treatments at the hospital, she said, "Come on, win one for me today, okay?"

As I was driving to work that day I said to myself, "That's it! That's what I'm going to do. I'm going to go out and win some races for Mom." And I did. I won three! When I called her back that evening and told her, she was really, really happy.

After that, I had a little extra vim and vigor in the mornings, and things started turning around. From then on, everything good started happening for me at the track. I decided to be positive for my mother's sake, instead of being negative because of my concern for her. I guess I drew some strength from the brave battle that my mom was fighting against her cancer, and winning races for her gave me a sense of purpose.

hings even got a little worse for Mom during the year, no doubt because of the chemotherapy. One day every month she would receive drug injections for eight hours. Her hair fell out and she had lots of bad side effects, like other illnesses caused by the drugs. Yet somehow, the fact that I was riding

well seemed to help her, too.

y the summer of 1987, the doctors operated on my mother again to see how much cancer remained inside her. Most of it was gone! They decided to give her radiation treatments. That was really hard on her.

The next season, I was back at Monmouth Park, riding better than ever. On one day, I won six races! Only three jockeys had ever done that in the history of Monmouth Park. A friend of mine called my mom after each race to tell her how I was doing.

"She won five," he told her. Then, "She won six." My mom had been having a rough day in the hospital, but when she got the phone call with that news, it made her feel a lot better.

And she did improve physically, too. Partway through the Monmouth season, she was between treatments and doing well. I was in contention for the Monmouth title—awarded to the jockey who rides more winners than any other. As soon as I took the season lead, I said, "Hurry, someone call and make a reservation for my mom so I can get her here tomorrow."

I wanted her to be with me while I was leading, so I had her come up from Florida. I think I won like five races one day, three the next day, and two another day. I won the season title, and she got better! She turned 50 last year, and she's still very much alive and spunky. She's even working with horses again. The doctors have found no further signs of cancer!

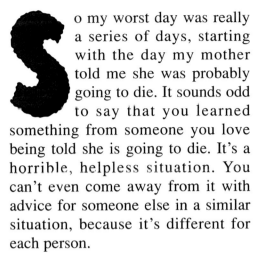

So my worst day was really a series of days, starting with the day my mother told me she was probably going to die. It sounds odd to say that you learned something from someone you love being told she is going to die. It's a horrible, helpless situation. You can't even come away from it with advice for someone else in a similar situation, because it's different for each person.

But I suppose I did learn some things. I learned, for the first time, that there are some things in life that you just can't fix. Until then, I could always think positively and fix anything in my life that went wrong. But my mother's cancer was something I could not control; I had to just let it run its course.

I also learned that your mother is your mother, no matter what. And no matter what's going on in her life, and how big her problems are, she wants to know what is going on in your life and wants to help you. I learned to share my life with her, no matter how trifling my problems seemed to be.

CHAPTER 8

GREG LEMOND

A hunting accident left the cyclist facing a long road back

 *illions of Americans ride bicycles, but only one, Greg LeMond, has ridden to the very top of the sport of cycling. As you might have guessed, it has been something of an uphill climb.*

Born in Lakewood, California, in 1961, Greg took up cycling at age 14 to strengthen his legs for skiing. He became fascinated by the two-wheeled sport and soon started racing—and winning—all over the United States. By age 19, Greg became a professional. In 1981, he moved to Europe and joined a top French team—something no American had ever done.

Two years later, Greg became the first American to win the pro road race at the world cycling championships. In 1984, he tackled the Tour

de France, the most important bicycle race in the world. Greg was only the second American to have attempted the Tour de France—and he finished third! Two years after that he won that grueling 23-day, 2,542-mile race through the mountains, countrysides, and cities of France. The first American to wear the famous yellow jersey, Greg was now an international hero!

Greg also won the Tour de France in 1989 and 1990. His victory in 1989 is considered by cycling experts to be the greatest achievement in the histo-

ry of that race, because Greg was 50 seconds behind the leader on the final day. No one had ever made up that big of a gap that late in the race.

That 1989 victory was also one of the greatest personal comeback stories in sports history. Two years earlier, on April 30, 1987, Greg was nearly killed in a hunting accident. Here is his account of his worst day.

y brother-in-law Patrick Blades, my uncle Rodney Barber, and I had gone turkey hunting on a ranch near Sacramento, California. To hunt turkeys, you have to go to a wooded area, because that's where turkeys hang out. Then you hide in the bushes, make some turkey-type noises, and wait for the big birds to show themselves. Patrick, my uncle, and I split up to find our own hunting places and, after a while, lost track of one another.

I found a spot that looked promising and I was just getting settled behind a bush when I heard a shot. I started to call out "Who shot...?" Then I looked down and saw that one of the fingers on my left hand was bleeding! When I stood up my entire left side hurt. I heard a strange noise coming from inside me: It sounded like I was breathing blood. I had been shot! I didn't realize how bad it was, but Patrick, who had fired the shot, just freaked out. My uncle heard the commotion and came running. He tried to calm both of us down.

We were hunting with shotguns, which shoot dozens of tiny metal pellets. The pellets spread out as soon as they leave the barrel of the gun. The spread, as it is called, gives you a better chance of hitting a moving target, like a bird, than does a single bullet. A small bird usually gets hit by only a few pellets. I'm a lot bigger than a bird; I got hit by about 50 pellets!

My uncle didn't tell me much about the moment I was shot until more than three years later. But I later learned that some of the pellets had gone through my neck, and blood spurted out of those wounds every time my heart beat. I had been hit in the kidney, liver, diaphragm, intestines, and, of course, the finger. Two pellets had lodged in the lining of my heart.

As I lay on the ground, thoughts of my life, my family, and my cycling career all flooded my mind. I remember thinking I just wanted to be able to see my wife, Kathy, and my son, Geoffrey (I've had two more children since), one more time. I didn't feel much pain, but I lost a lot of blood and went into shock.

uckily, a police helicopter had been sent to an automobile accident nearby and when none of the victims needed help, the members of the helicopter crew decided to check out our hunting accident. If they hadn't come by, I probably would have died from the loss of blood. It was that bad.

They flew me to the hospital at the University of California at Davis. The surgeon was waiting when I arrived. She looked over all my wounds and said she thought that I would recover completely. But it was going to take a lot of work.

The surgeon removed 20 pellets from different parts of my body, but there are about 30 more still remaining in me. I had lost about two pints of blood and my entire body was swollen with inflammation. After a while, scar tissue developed around the pellets that remained in my body so they were no longer a danger, but at first, my body did not like having them there.

During those first days, I learned a lot about pain. I never thought I would be the type of person who needed painkillers. After all, I pushed myself hard while training and racing in cycling. But the suffering you feel on your bike is nothing compared with real pain. After the accident, I would walk around my bedroom and just cry and cry because it hurt so much.

It was very difficult to come back. In fact, the doctors tell me that my right lung still has not completely recovered from the accident, even though it happened nearly four years ago.

That first week, just walking to the toilet was like taking on a mountain in the Tour de France. But my body healed at a fast rate. I had lost about 15 pounds, mostly muscle, but in four or five weeks, I worked myself back to the point where I could train. I went out rid-ing, but my stomach was weak. Before the accident, I was used to training as much as seven hours a day! But my first ride after the accident ended in an hour. I went home and just laid on the couch. The human body has a remarkable ability to recover and it seemed to have come back to a certain level fairly quickly. But it hadn't come back enough for me to be a competitive rider yet.

Then I had more complications related to the accident: Less than three months after the shooting, I had an intestinal blockage, and in July I

had to have my appendix removed. That surgery finished off any hope I had of competing during the 1987 racing season.

Although all the physical problems set me back, it was my pride that almost finished me off. Early in 1988, I was back training and trying to get ready to race in Europe. It was a big mistake. None of the pro teams wanted to take me on. Everyone said I would never be able to come back. As the summer progressed, I felt as if people were laughing at me. I had already won the Tour de France, in 1986, and some of my rivals from that year were enjoying seeing me take a fall now. That made me feel that I had to rush things to show all those people that I could still do it.

Then in July 1988, I injured my shin in a cycling crash and had to have more surgery. I had to start from scratch a third time. I don't think any other rider has ever had to come back from so many frustrating setbacks, but I didn't think about that. I just took everything one day at a time. In the fall, I started training again.

IN 1989, GREG WON THE TOUR DE FRANCE FOR THE SECOND TIME, BECOMING THE FIRST RIDER IN THE HISTORY OF THE TOUR TO MAKE UP A 50 SECOND MARGIN ON THE FINAL DAY OF THE RACE. AND IN 1990, HE WON HIS THIRD TOUR DE FRANCE.

By the next spring, I did okay in several races in Europe and came home to the U.S. to ride in the first Tour de Trump, an 837-mile, 10-day race from Albany, New York, to Richmond, Virginia. I thought I had recovered fully and that I could win the race. Instead, I finished 27th! I was just not capable of staying with the other riders when we were racing on the hills. I suffered unbelievably. I grew depressed, and I began to doubt myself.

The hardest thing about coming back from an injury is that you always remember yourself at your best. You never remember the way you were when things went badly. I kept flashing back to how I rode in the '86 Tour de France, when I floated up hills and rode 30 miles per hour for an hour and a half during the time trials. Those thoughts made it difficult for me to accept the way I was riding now, even though it was good for someone who had almost died two years earlier!

I was putting in a lot of training, and I felt I wasn't getting anywhere. I began to think that maybe I wouldn't be able to come back, after all.

The Tour of Italy is a major race held in June that I wanted to use to prepare for the Tour de France. But once again, I really struggled during parts of it. During a break in the race, I had a blood test and the doctor told me I was anemic. That meant my blood didn't have enough iron in it. I don't know if it was related to the accident or if I had just been pushing myself too hard. But I knew that being anemic might explain why I felt so run down and made so little progress. The doctor gave me a couple of shots of iron, and I felt stronger. At last, my body felt as if it had recovered to the point where I could push it again. And I did.

Most people didn't expect me to do much at the Tour de France that July. Even I figured that finishing in the Top 20 would be a good performance. The Tour consists of a number of shorter races that together form the total race. On the first day, I took fourth place. That was a good start, I thought. A few days later I took over the yellow jersey, which is worn by the cyclist who is leading the overall race. That's when I felt I had a chance to win.

Still, the cycling over the mountains was hard. I lost my lead in the Pyrenees, but gained it back in the Alps. I lost it again, but came back to win the race on the final day when I made up 50 seconds during a 15.2-mile sprint to the finish.

On the victory platform, I thought about the previous two years, about how I had almost quit racing and what a good thing it was that I never give up early. That's one thing that the whole experience has taught me: Never give up early.

There were other lessons that came

from my worst day. Probably the most important thing I learned is that you have to make every day count. When you come as close to dying as I did, you realize that every day is precious and that you should take advantage of it.

I still want to be successful and I'm willing to do what it takes to do well in cycling, but I'm no longer willing to devote my life 100 percent to cycling. I want to enjoy my family and all the other things that life has to offer. I can't act as if life is going to go on forever the same as it has been going.

The day I got shot began a year and a half of incredible frustration for me. But I believe that everything that has happened, happened for the best. The hunting accident, the surgeries, the long struggle to come back—I've turned them all into positives in my life.

CHAPTER 9

KARL MALONE

Karl thought he was hot stuff until poor grades knocked him off the court

arl Malone, the star forward for the Utah Jazz of the National Basketball Association, is nicknamed The Mailman because he always delivers. Game in and game out, his teammates can depend on him to produce points, rebounds, and dedicated defense. In his first six professional seasons, 1985-86 to 1990-91, Karl delivered an average of 25.6 points and 10.8 rebounds per game. And he missed only three games in those six years!

During the 1989-90 season, his best, Karl became the ninth NBA player in history to average 30 or more points and 10 or more rebounds in the same season. He led the Jazz in scoring in 73 of their 82 games, poured in a career-high 61 points one night, and finished with an average of 31 points and 11.1 rebounds per game. Michael Jordan was the only other NBA player to score more points per game than Karl! The Mailman kept on rolling through the 1990-91 season, averaging 29 points and 11.8 rebounds.

Karl grew up in tiny Summerfield, Louisiana, the second youngest of nine children. His dad left the family when Karl was young. His mom,

Shirley, worked in the sawmills and in the poultry houses of northern Louisiana, often putting in two shifts a day, until she met and married Ed Turner in 1975. They opened a grocery store, and made sure that the kids behaved.

Karl played basketball and studied elementary education at Louisiana Technical University, a college that had been better known for its women's basketball than for it's men's team. In 1982-83, he became the first player in the history of the Southland Conference to be named Player of the Year and Newcomer of the Year in the same season. The next two seasons, he led Louisiana Tech to the NCAA Tournament.

In 1985, the Jazz made Karl the 13th pick in the NBA draft. He made an immediate impression, averaging 14.9 points and 8.9 rebounds as a rookie. By 1989, the 6'9", 255-pound forward was the Most Valuable Player of the NBA All-Star Game!

Karl has gone from being a high school star to one of the best basketball players in the world. But before

he could make that leap, one day, May 15, 1981, when he was 17 years old, he had to have all the air let out of his basketball dreams.

I was a senior at Summerfield High School, and our basketball team had won the Class C Louisiana State championship for the third straight year. Class C is for the smallest high schools in the state and ours sure was small. There were only 11 kids in the entire senior class! That made us especially proud of winning the state title. People from other towns used to say to us, "You guys are just a lot of country farm boys, and you'll never win the state championship." We showed them. We won it the last three years I was in high school!

I was pretty much full-grown by the time I was 14 years old, so I was a big star. My senior year, I had averaged 37 points and 27 rebounds during the season, and was named to the McDonald's All-America team. A lot of major colleges had recruited me; they all wanted me to play basketball for them. Everybody told me that I was going to play in the NBA some day. I had decided to go to Louisiana

YOUR GRADES ARE SO BAD THAT YOU WON'T BE ELIGIBLE TO PLAY BASKETBALL DURING YOUR FIRST YEAR OF COLLEGE.

GRADES

LATER THAT AFTERNOON, KARL TOLD HIS MOTHER THAT HE WOULD HAVE TO SPEND HIS FIRST YEAR AT COLLEGE STUDYING TO GET HIS GRADES BACK UP.. NO BASKETBALL FOR A WHOLE YEAR.

WHAT AM I GOING TO DO NOW?

KARL, YOU HAVE TO WORK FOR WHAT YOU WANT IN LIFE. NO ONE IS GOING TO HAND IT TO YOU.

NO ONE IS GOING TO LIKE ME IF I'M NOT A BASKETBALL STAR.

Tech because I wanted to stay close to home, and Tech is only 39 miles from Summerfield. I was ready to be a big star in college, too.

y the spring of my senior year in high school, I had become pretty cocky. I knew I was good and nobody could tell me otherwise. I was a big hero at Summerfield High. It got so I was beginning to think that I was better than other people; that I was special. I was so caught up in myself that I didn't respect other people, or care much about their feelings.

I didn't listen to my teachers or do my schoolwork. We lived out in the woods, and I would come home on Friday afternoon, throw down my books, and spend the weekend hunting and fishing. Then I'd get up early Monday and do a little bit of homework. I think sometimes officials at school looked the other way because I was such a good athlete. That just made me believe even more strongly that I could do anything I wanted.

Then I had my worst day. I was sitting in science class when the principal, Mr. Scriber, came to get me. I

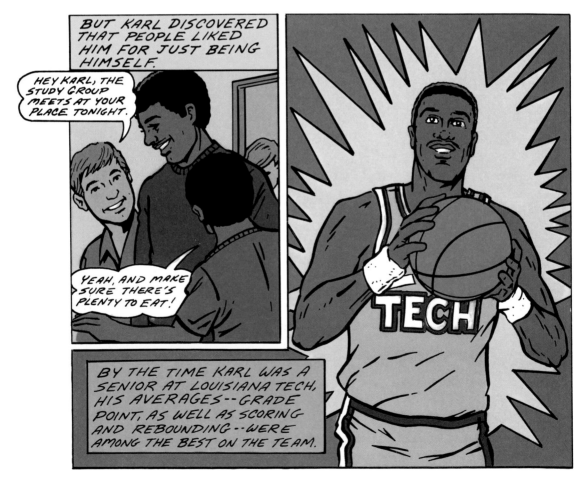

knew that something was wrong because he had walked all the way down the hall from his office. He wouldn't do that if he had just wanted to chat!

Mr. Scriber was real quiet as we walked back to his office. "What is it?" I wondered. "He made that long walk to get me, so it must be important." Then he told me that my grades were so bad—I had a 1.99 grade point average, out of a possible 4—that I would not be eligible to play basketball during my first year at college!

Mr. Scriber told me I would have to spend that first year at Louisiana Tech improving my grades. "Either this will make you a better person," he said, "or you will be back home real soon cutting lumber for the local paper mills."

I was scared. I knew about cutting lumber. My mother had worked for years in those mills, and I had seen what the men did in those places. It was *hard* work. It was definitely not what I had in mind for my future.

t home that afternoon, my mother noticed my long face and asked me what was going on. I sat down, hung my head, and told her what Mr. Scriber had said. "What am I going to do now?" I asked her.

My mom told me my only choice was to go to college and work hard to improve my grades. I thought maybe if she would send me to summer school, I could get my grades up; and then I would be allowed to play. But she said no. She said I had made my own bed and now I had to lie in it. In other words, I had to face the fact that I had messed up, and I must work my way out of the mess by myself.

y mother told me that things like this always happen for the best. She said it was time for me to learn that you have got to go out and work hard for what you want in life. Nobody is going to hand it to you on a silver platter, she said.

Basketball had always come easily to me, partly because I was so big. Passing on from one grade to the next had never been a problem, either. My mom said I had to realize that life didn't always work that way. It wasn't always so easy.

Still, I was stunned. I thought the only reason I was going to college was to play basketball. Now, suddenly, I wasn't a basketball star any more. I was just another student. And a bad one!

I moped around all summer. I wasn't angry about not being able to play basketball, because I realized that it was no one's fault but my own. But I was afraid. I thought people wouldn't like me anymore because I wasn't a basketball star. I didn't think they would accept me as just another human being. And what if I couldn't get my grades up? Sometimes I thought I didn't even want to go to college if I couldn't play basketball.

But I did go, and by the end of my first week at college, I realized that people *did* care about me as a person, even if I wasn't a basketball star. I met other students who liked me for just being me. They didn't care if I played basketball or not.

I also talked to Assistant Coach Tommy Joe Eagles soon after I got to Tech. He said that God wouldn't put hurdles in front of you that you can't jump over. That helped me a lot. It gave me confidence that I could do what I had to do.

There were other people like Coach Eagles, who also wanted to help me. So I decided to help myself. I said to myself, "I want to be a better person, and I'll do whatever it takes to become one."

I started to crack the books, and I got my grades up. I began listening to other people, especially my mother. I started to say, "Yes, ma'am," and "No, ma'am," and do the other things that show respect for other people.

My view of the world changed after my worst day. It seemed that my whole life had somehow slowed down, because, for the first time in a long time, I realized that there was more to life than basketball and that there are higher powers in the world

than Karl Malone. Before that day in May, I thought that I was "The Stuff" and that anything I did was okay. No one had ever told me, "You can't do that."

aving basketball taken away really humbled me. I learned that I wasn't so special and that things would not always just come to me. Instead, I was going to have to go out and work hard for what I wanted to get in life.

In college, that meant mostly working hard at my studies. Since I've been in the NBA, it has meant taking care of myself physically by eating right, lifting weights, running, and working on my game. I don't think I would be such a hard worker today if I had not had my bad day back then.

I also learned that instead of being so caught up in myself, I should respect and care about other people. Now I know that if you make yourself a better person, you'll make yourself a better player, too.

Oh, and guess what? By my fourth year at Louisiana Tech, my grade point average was among the best on the basketball team. And my scoring and rebounding averages were tops, too!

CHAPTER 10

SHIRLEY MULDOWNEY

A freak accident left drag racing's queen unable to walk, let alone drive

S hirley Muldowney holds every record for women in profes-sional drag racing, as well as many records for all drag racers—male and female. Clearly, she is the best female drag racer in the history of the sport. She is so remarkable, in fact, that a full-length feature movie, called "Heart like a Wheel," was made about her!

In drag racing, pairs of cars race each other over one fourth of a mile. In the top classes of competition, the cars are long and skinny with tiny front tires and big, fat rear tires. These 4,500-horsepower dragsters can reach speeds of just under 300 miles per hour in about five seconds. "It's like having a tiger by the tail!" Shirley says.

Shirley grew up in Schenectady, New York, and first became interested in drag racing when she was 15.

By 17, Shirley was already a wife and a mother. At 19, she became a professional racer and one of the very first women in the sport.

Over the years, Shirley worked her way up the ladder of drag racing. In 1973, she began competing at the highest level, which is called Top Fuel. She was the first woman ever licensed to compete in that class. Since then, she has won 18 races in national competition, more than all other female drivers combined.

Shirley won the National Hot Rod Association's Top Fuel world championship in 1977. In 1980, she became the first two-time winner of that title, and in 1982, she won it a third time. A five-time All-America, she shares the record for an unbroken string of Nationals victories (three). Shirley was 49 years old when she won her 18th Nationals race in 1989 and, as this book went to print, she was looking for a sponsor so she could begin her 34th year of racing.

"Heart like a Wheel" was made in 1982, two years before Shirley had her worst day. That day was June 24, 1984. The story of what happened to Shirley then, and in the months that followed, would make a fascinating movie, too. Here's how Shirley tells it.

t was the first day of qualifying at Sanair Speedway, a racetrack near Montreal, Canada. I was at the starting line for the last race of the afternoon. My son, John, who has been one of my mechanics since he was 14, wished me good luck, and the pit crew looked over the car one more time. I watched the yellow light, waiting for it to turn green—my signal to go.

When the light changed, I stepped on the fuel pedal and took off.

Within a few seconds, I was speeding along at 247 miles per hour. Then the inner tube in my left front tire popped out of its casing. That happens sometimes when you are racing that fast. Usually, you can just keep driving on the wheel rim. But this time, I saw the tube wrap itself around the axle. Suddenly, the front wheels locked up. The car left the course at a 90 degree turn and went head-on into a ditch!

When the car hit the far side of the ditch, it broke into pieces. One piece was the driver's seat, with me still strapped in it! I bounced and flew about 600 feet into an open field. The seat has a "roll cage" around it to protect the driver during an accident. But the part of the cage that was supposed to cover my legs had broken off!

I remember hitting the ground twice, and then I guess I was unconscious for a minute or two. The next thing I knew, I was on my side looking at the grass and the sky. I was still strapped into my seat, and the safety

THE BONES IN HER LEGS WERE SHATTERED BY THE CRASH.

WE DID ALL WE COULD, BUT I DON'T KNOW IF SHE'LL BE ABLE TO WALK AGAIN.

hoop, fortunately, still surrounded my head. I opened my eyes and was amazed that I was alive. I thought I had been thrown from the car, which is usually fatal. But I hadn't been thrown from the car. The car had simply disintegrated during the crash!

eople were all around me, trying to figure out how badly I was hurt. I felt terrible pain. The bones in my legs had been shattered, and the rest of my body was in pretty bad shape, too.

One finger was nearly severed and three more were broken. My pelvis was also broken. I was covered with mud and grass and grease. I kept saying to my boyfriend, Rahn Tobler, "I'm really in trouble. I'm really in trouble."

An ambulance took me to the hospital. But before the doctors could operate, the hospital staff spent six hours cleaning the dirt and grease out of my wounds with wire brushes and a special kind of sterile water. The surgery took another six hours. Afterward, I was still in unbelievable pain.

It was four months before I could move anything below my waist. I

spent two months in the hospital in Montreal and then went home to Michigan and spent more time in a hospital there. I had several more operations and was in terrible pain much of the time.

For more than a year, I had to rely on other people to do *everything* for me. I couldn't fix my own meals or do my own shopping or even take a bath without help. I couldn't walk and I was in a wheelchair for a long while. That depressed me a lot. It's very tough being that dependent on other people. And I hated being cooped up in the house. I'm used to moving fast!

I wanted to be on my own again, and for me, racing is a great symbol of independence. I knew better than anyone just how dangerous drag racing could be, but I also knew that racing was what made me feel happy and alive. It's kind of crazy. Here I was, struggling to drive a wheelchair around my home without banging up the furniture, and I was starting to think that I wanted to race again. My doctor just couldn't understand my desire to get back to racing, but I knew that for me it was important.

About seven months after the accident, in January 1985, I went to a doctor who specializes in injuries to race-car drivers. He was able to fix my injuries so that I could begin to walk again. (But I had to give up high heeled shoes, which I love, forever.) With this new doctor's help and with

Rahn's encouragement, I began to feel hopeful that I could race again.

I had what I needed: a goal. I stopped feeling depressed, and I started working harder at getting better. I continued to have a lot of pain in my left leg and foot. And because of the way the bones had healed, my right leg was an inch shorter than the left, so it took a lot of hard work to learn to walk again.

I took physical therapy with special trainers for an hour and a half every day. I didn't like the physical therapy; it also hurt like crazy! But I went, and I worked out with weights and did exercises when I was home. I pushed myself to do those things because I knew I had to do them if I wanted to get well and strong again.

It took a lot of hard work, sweat, and tears, but I *did* get better. By January 1986, I was back in the driver's seat, competing! I made my return, a year and a half after the accident, at Firebird International Raceway in Phoenix, Arizona, and in 1989, I won another national race!

My worst day led to about 18 awful months, but there were good things that happened because of it. I discovered how many wonderful things I had in my life: friends, fans, and people who truly cared about me.

Rahn's support through all those miserable months was unbelievable. (We finally got married in 1988.) My son, John, was great, too. But it wasn't just those who were close to me: After the accident, I received about 4,500 fan letters! Also, other people in racing expressed their concern. I realized that even though we were intense competitors on the track, they were friends who would come to my aid when I needed them. Being a woman in a man's sport, I didn't always feel accepted. After my worst day I learned that I *did* have the support of the racing community when I needed it.

I also learned how much having a goal can help you motivate yourself. Right after the accident, I was happy just to be alive. But soon, I got bored and frustrated with life. I couldn't do much, and I didn't think there was a point in pushing myself to get better because I didn't have anything to work toward.

Once I had my goal to race again, I was able to force myself to work hard toward a complete recovery. Getting out of that wheelchair became much more important when it was the first step toward racing again. I could never have made myself go through all the pain of physical therapy just so I could go shopping again.

ainly, though, my worst day taught me to be patient. In drag racing, everything happens quickly. The starting light turns green, you step on the pedal, and less than five seconds later, the race is over.

I'd been used to moving fast in many parts of my life. I started racing when I was a 15, I got married the first time at 16, I had a baby when I was 17. I was always kind of impatient; I wanted things to happen immediately.

It's easy to forget that some things must take a long time. Healing is one of those things, especially when you are recuperating from an accident as serious as the one I had. You just don't get instant results. You have to work for a long, long time to get your reward. So I was forced to learn patience—and I did. I stayed with it and worked hard, until I reached my goal. And my reward was to go fast again!

CHAPTER 11

MARTINA NAVRATILOVA

After an upset loss, young Martina feared that her tennis career was over

 artina Navratilova grew up in Revnice [zhev-NEE-za], Czechoslovakia, a small town outside the capital, Prague. She started hanging around tennis courts when she was five years old and at 15, she won the national championship for women.

In 1973, Martina was playing and winning tournaments in the United States and in Europe. But the Czech Tennis Federation restricted her travel to tournaments, forcing Martina to make a very difficult decision. As she left to play in the 1975 U.S. Open, 18-year-old Martina decided to defect—to live in the U.S. without the Czech government's permission.

"I was going out to conquer the world," Martina recalled. "I didn't realize how big the world was!"

As big as the world proved to be, Martina conquered it. Since 1977, she has finished the season ranked no lower than Number 3 among women tennis players in the world, and seven times she was ranked Number 1 for the year. Entering 1991, Martina held the record for the most match victories in a row, with 74, and had won 153 singles titles in her career, second only to Chris Evert.

Among those titles are the 18 that Martina has won at tennis's four most important tournaments, the Grand Slam events. Those championships include a record nine wins at Wimbledon in England, four at the U.S. Open, three at the Australian Open, and two at the French Open.

Martina is also the most successful doubles player in the history of tennis. She and Pam Shriver formed a doubles team that from 1981 through 1990 won 89 titles, including 20 in Grand Slam events.

But Martina has had a strong influence on the women's game beyond the numbers of titles won. In 1981, she learned to eat properly and started a program of overall physical training, which many younger tennis players have also adopted.

They also have emulated her powerful style of play, which is built around a 90-mile-per-hour serve and a rush up to the net to hit lightning fast volleys (hitting the ball before it touches the court) at her opponents. That style is different from the style played by Chris Evert and other female stars of the early 1980s, who stayed back near the baseline, or back-line, of the court.

AS A RISING YOUNG TENNIS STAR IN CZECHOSLOVAKIA, 16-YEAR-OLD MARTINA DREAMED OF THE DAY WHEN SHE'D PLAY IN A MAJOR TOURNAMENT IN THE UNITED STATES.

THE CZECH TENNIS FEDERATION IS SENDING YOU TO THE U.S. OPEN. BUT YOU'LL HAVE TO TRAVEL ALONE.

THIS IS A DREAM COME TRUE!

Martina has had plenty of success against "baseliners." But she remembers one day early in her career when one of these baseliners made her think that her career was over. The day was August 30, 1973; the place was Forest Hills, New York.

There have been a few bad days over the years, but the worst day I ever had was when I was 16 years old. I was playing in my very first U.S. Open; in fact, it was my first major appearance in the United States.

For years, I had dreamed of playing tennis in the U.S. I had an uncle who lived in Canada, and he sent me tennis magazines. Sitting in the small apartment I shared with my parents and sister, I would read about the great stars, such as Rod Laver and Billie Jean King. More than anything, I wanted to play like—and with—them.

Finally, in the winter of 1973, the Czech Tennis Federation decided to let me and another woman play eight tournaments in the United States. I was thrilled! At that time, most Czech people could not travel out-

BEFORE THE U.S. OPEN, MARTINA PLAYED IN A TOURNAMENT IN TORONTO, CANADA. SHE MADE IT TO THE THIRD ROUND, AND EVERYONE -- INCLUDING MARTINA'S IDOL, ROD LAVER--THOUGHT SHE WAS GOING TO BE A STAR.

I THINK WE'LL SEE GREAT THINGS FROM MARTINA NAVRATILOVA SOMEDAY.

NOW I *KNOW* I'M GOOD!

TOMORROWS MATCHES

M. NAVRATILOVA vs V. BURTON

TOMORROW'S WIN WILL BE AN EASY ONE. I'M THE BETTER PLAYER AND I'VE ALREADY BEATEN VERONICA BURTON THIS YEAR.

HER BACKHAND IS MUCH STRONGER THAN I THOUGHT.

side the country at all. Many things in our lives were controlled by the Communist government, so this was a special treat. Never mind that I spoke almost no English and I would get only $11 a day for food and other personal expenses: I was going to the United States!

I made a good showing on the tour that winter—I even reached the semifinal of one tournament! After spending the rest of the winter at home, I played several big tournaments in Europe. At the French Open, I made the quarterfinal. Then I won a couple of matches at Wimbledon.

When the Federation sent me to America again that summer, I was ready. First I played in a tournament in Toronto, Canada. Not only did I make it to the third round, but my idol, Rod Laver, saw one of my matches and actually told people that he thought I was going to be a good player! Now I *knew* I was good. I couldn't wait to play in the U.S. Open, America's most important tournament.

I was traveling alone that summer. There were no other Czechs in the

women's tournament at the Open, and I had no family or coach with me. I didn't really know any of the women on the tour because I was so new. It was hard for me to make friends because I was young and I spoke so little English. But I was excited about playing in the Open.

These days, the Open is played on hard, cement courts at the United States Tennis Association National Tennis Center in Flushing Meadows, New York. But in 1973, it was played on grass courts at the West Side Tennis Club in Forest Hills, New York. I was used to playing on clay courts; the courts I learned on in Czechoslovakia were clay.

In tennis, the surface you are playing on makes a big difference because the ball reacts differently and the players can't move around the court the same way. Clay is slow and slippery. Grass surfaces are slick and fast. It takes a while to learn how to play well on it. This was my first year of playing on grass, and I really didn't know what I was doing.

For my first match at the Open, I was up against a girl from England named Veronica Burton. Veronica was 21 and had been a junior champion in England. I beat her earlier that year, and my record was better than hers. I also had a more powerful game: I could serve and volley well. Veronica was a baseliner. I knew that I could do a lot more up at the net than Veronica could do from way back there. So I was cocky. I felt I was the better player and that I could beat Veronica easily.

But I didn't beat her. I lost.

Right from the start of the match, I did everything wrong. Veronica had grown up playing on grass courts, because they are very common in England, so she knew what she was doing out there. I didn't take that into consideration before the match.

Nor did I use the right strategy. My forehand stroke was stronger than my backhand, so I assumed that everyone in the world had a weak backhand. I kept attacking Veronica's. But it turned out that she had a better backhand than forehand. The more I hit balls to that side, the better she liked it!

I lost the match, 5-7, 6-1, 6-3. And the worst thing was that in the third set, I was leading in every game, and I still lost! I was devastated! I thought my career was over. I was only 16 years old and had just started to play on the international level, but I decided right then it was hopeless. I thought I would never be any good if I could lose to that girl!

I went back to the locker room, took a long, cold shower, and cried my little heart out. I had no one to talk to about how I felt. My family was thousands of miles away in Czechoslovakia. I couldn't talk to any other players. I had nothing to do except think about the match and cry.

79

Until that match, I had thought that I could be one of the top players in the world. But that loss seemed so terrible that I forgot all that.

I played one more tournament in the States and then went home to Czechoslovakia, as scheduled. I continued playing tennis, because it was what my family and the Czech Tennis Federation expected of me. I didn't have time to dwell on my loss too much. I had so many things to do: I went to school and I played tennis.

he devastation I felt when I lost to Veronica passed with time. In fact, it probably helped that I was still playing tennis. I won some matches and I found out that I wasn't really that bad. It helped me feel less discouraged.

So by the next year, when I went back out on the international circuit, I was ready to go out again and try to prove myself. And I did! When I went to the United States the following winter, I won my first professional tournament, the Virginia Slims of Orlando, Florida. I continued to improve. By 1975, I was among the Top 5 female players in the world, and I've gone on to have a great career.

ut I'll never forget the way I felt that August day in 1973. I have probably had even greater losses since then, when I failed in matches that everybody expected me to win, but I never thought after any of those losses that my career was over. I have no idea why it happened that one day and never again. Maybe it was because I was only 16. Or perhaps it was that I was all alone in a foreign land and playing in a very big tournament.

But I do know that I learned an important lesson from that day. It taught me that one match doesn't make you a loser—or a true player either. It works both ways. You can't let *one* contest take on too much importance. If you get cocky after a single win or depressed after a single loss, you will never succeed because you won't be ready to face your next challenge. Either you will be too confident to prepare fully, or you will be too upset to play well.

As my worst day taught me, how you do in one match really isn't that important. It's what you do over the long run that counts.

CHAPTER 12

MARY DECKER SLANEY

Mary's long-held Olympic dream came crashing down on the track

ary Decker Slaney is the most successful female middle-distance runner the United States has ever produced. From 1973 through 1985, she set American records for every distance from 800 meters through 10,000 meters. She also set five world records, including three in the prestigious mile run, from 1980-85.

Despite all her success, Mary has never won a medal in the Olympics. A leg injury kept her off the U.S. team in 1976. Although she made the team easily in 1980, the U.S. team did not go to the Games. The Olympics were to be held in the Soviet capital of Moscow, and President Jimmy Carter asked the U.S. Olympic Committee to boycott—or stay away from—the Games because the Soviet Union had invaded another country, Afghanistan. Again, Mary watched the Games on TV.

Finally, on August 10, 1984, Mary's dream of running in the Olympics came true when she stepped to the starting line for the final of the 3,000-meter race in Los Angeles, California. Little did Mary know her dream would turn into a nightmare. Here's how she recalls the worst day she ever had.

It was the first Olympic race that I'd ever been able to compete in, so I was really excited. The newspaper and television reporters had all built up the race as a big duel between me and Zola Budd.

Zola was an 18-year-old South African. She had obtained British citizenship a few months before the Olympics, which enabled her to participate in the Games. (South Africans were not allowed to compete in the Olympics because of their country's apartheid policy, which separated black people from white people.) Zola was a good runner. In January, she had broken my world record in the 5,000 meters. So I guess a lot of track fans were excited about seeing us race each other.

It really wasn't a personal duel between us at all, though. We had never raced each other; we had never even met. Besides, I was a big favorite among fans because of my past performances and because the Olympics were being held in my home country. I considered Maricica Puică my main competition in the race. Maricica had competed at the Olympics in 1980 and 1984. She

held the current world record in the mile and was the world cross-country champion.

Finally, the race began, and I took the lead for the first few laps. But I didn't want to go out too quickly. So when Zola came up beside me and began to pass, I thought, "Well, that's good. She can help with the work." Leading a race gets tiring; it's easier to run a little bit behind, on the shoulder of another person.

As Zola passed me, she moved into my path. Usually, when you pass someone, you run past them completely and then you move over to the inside of the track. Zola moved over as she was passing. I should have let her know that she was cutting me off. Normally, I would touch the runner or something so she doesn't cut in quite so soon. But I didn't do that because of the pre-race press hype. If I touched Zola, I thought, people would say I was shoving her or something. Maybe the whole incident could have been avoided if I had been just a little more defensive. But I wasn't, and since the other runners were beside

me and behind me, I had nowhere to go. I could not get out of Zola's way. My legs got tangled up with her foot, and I fell.

s soon as I hit the ground and rolled over, I tried to get up and back into the race. But I couldn't! It was like I was tied to the ground. Then I felt a terrible pain in my hip. That's when it hit me that I wasn't going to be able to finish the race. I began to cry. I cried because my hip hurt and because I was upset and because I

was disappointed. A lot of work over a lot of years and a lot of dreams went down with me when I fell.

After that, I remember watching legs go by and seeing track officials standing over me. It seemed like ages before my fiancé (now my husband), Richard Slaney, came and picked me up. Maricica won the race and Zola finished seventh.

We went straight to the hospital and had an X-ray taken. There wasn't major damage, but the soft tissue in my hip would take time to heal.

As it turned out, it took 12 weeks for my hip to heal. I had trouble

standing up and sitting down and getting in and out of cars. I couldn't run, so I learned how to knit. I enjoyed the knitting. It gave me time to think.

A lot was written in the press and stated on TV about what had happened in that Olympic race—especially about whether I was tripped or not. I was also criticized heavily for crying. My feelings were hurt by that. But, I got a lot of sympathetic fan mail, and that helped.

As time passed, I began to get over the disappointment of failing to finish my first Olympic race. In fact, I think taking the fall made me a stronger person. I believe that things happen for a reason. You don't always know the reason, and you don't always know how much time will pass before you understand why something bad happened. But, often, a bad experience can make you a better person. I think I came out of my worst day as a tougher athlete.

When things don't go your way, all you can do is work harder and keep aiming toward your goals. If one bad day makes you give up those goals, you will never succeed. No matter how rough things seem to get, whether it's in sports or school or music lessons, you just have to hang in there. Sometimes it takes a long time for things to get better, but they *do* get better.

I went into the 1985 summer track season extremely determined to have a successful season. And I had the best season of my entire career! I won all of the races I entered. I beat every runner who had been in that Olympic race—including Zola and Maricica.

That season, I set a world record for the mile, and American records in the 800, 1,000, 3,000, and 5,000 meters. I almost set a record in the 1,500 too. I wanted to prove to myself that I was as good as anyone who had been in the Olympic race. And I did. Nobody will ever know if I would have won that race had I completed it, but at least I showed myself that I was as good as the women who had.

I made it to the Olympics in Seoul, South Korea, in 1988, but it was hard. I had taken 1986 off to have a baby, and I had missed the 1987 season and the first few months of 1988 with injuries. At Seoul, I ended up finishing eighth in the 1,500 meters and 10th in the 3,000 meters. I was disappointed, but I didn't cry in public. I managed to go on from there with hopes of doing better at the 1992 Games in Barcelona, Spain.

When something like that fall I had in the Olympics happens, it hurts. The physical pain goes away soon, and the emotional pain goes away after a while, too. But the strength you gain from the experience lasts the rest of your life.

CHAPTER 13

HERSCHEL WALKER

Eleven-year-old Herschel faked an injury rather than risk losing a race

Ever since he came out of a small town in Georgia to set a national college rushing record for freshmen in 1980, Herschel Junior Walker has been one of the most famous and successful running backs in football. His combination of size, strength, and speed have fascinated football fans and excited football coaches.

Unlike most football players, Herschel doesn't lift weights, and unlike most people, he doesn't sleep more than four hours a night nor eat three meals a day. But at 6'1" and 225 pounds, he has the muscles of a bodybuilder and the quick feet of a track sprinter. He developed that body mostly by doing sit-ups, push-ups, wind sprints, and giving a complete effort in everything he does.

Herschel grew up in Wrightsville,

Georgia. At Johnson County High School, he set national high school records for touchdowns in a season, with 45 his senior year, and in a career, with 86, and led his team to the Class A state championship.

As a freshman at the University of Georgia, he rushed for 1,616 yards, and helped the Bulldogs win the national football championship. Two years later, he won the Heisman Trophy, given each year to the nation's *best football player. By that time, Herschel had set ten National Collegiate Athletic Association (NCAA) records and 30 University of Georgia records. His 5,259 yards rushing is still third on the all-time NCAA list.*

After his junior year, Herschel left college to play three seasons with the New Jersey Generals of the United States Football League, a new professional football league. His total of 2,411 yards in 1985 set a record that still stands for the most yards rushing in one season by any pro football player in history!

The USFL folded after that season, and Herschel joined the Dallas Cowboys of the National Football League. In 1987, he became the first NFL player to gain 700 yards in both rushing and receiving in the same year, and in 1988, he became the 10th player in history to gain more than 2,000 yards from scrimmage. Traded to the Minnesota Vikings for five players in 1989, Herschel has led the Vikings in rushing the last two seasons.

But Herschel was not always a star athlete. In fact, he remembers one of his first attempts to prove himself as an athlete. It was in the spring of 1973, when Herschel was 11 years old, and it was the worst day he ever had.

 was in the fifth grade at Johnson County Elementary School, and it was late spring, just before school let out for the summer. Every year, at the end of the school year, we would have a kind of field day, when all the kids would compete in different sports events.

I wasn't athletic as a little kid. People can't believe that I was once little and slow, but I remember. I was a runt! Everyone at school thought it was cool if you were athletic, but I wasn't.

That spring, I started thinking about the sports day. I knew that among the events was going to be a one-mile run for the students in my grade. I thought that if I could win that one-mile run, I would be a hero at school. It would show that I was athletic, and then everyone would think I was cool. I really wanted them to think that.

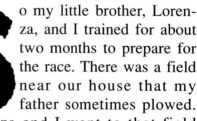 o my little brother, Lorenza, and I trained for about two months to prepare for the race. There was a field near our house that my father sometimes plowed. Lorenza and I went to that field almost every day, and we would run and run and run. We didn't know anything about training for a race, but we figured if we ran a lot we would get faster. I really worked hard to get ready for that race. I knew that by the time race day came, I would be ready to run fast, and I'd win.

The day came, and was I excited. I knew I was ready. Finally, it was time to run. We had to go four laps around a big track, just like in a real track meet. There was a bunch of kids running in the race, but everyone expected one guy, Willie Jenkins, to win. He was one of those athletic kids, and he was a fast runner. Everyone knew that.

The race began, and I was doing well. I was running right with Willie! I knew I had prepared myself well for the race, but I was surprised when I saw that I could actually keep up with the fastest kid in the class. But after the first lap, my mind started thinking, "You're not going to win this race." Even though I was in the lead, I said to myself, "Herschel, you don't know how to

win this race. You might as well quit now." It wasn't that I felt I was going to get tired or anything, it was just something in my mind that made me doubt my ability. Suddenly, all the confidence I had before the race was gone.

But I kept running anyway. During the third lap, I was still doing very well—better than I'd ever done in a race before. I couldn't believe it! Instead of being really excited and encouraged by how well I was doing, though, I was

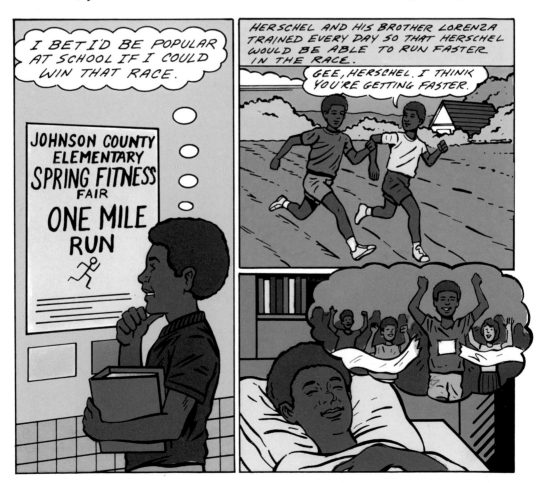

even more certain that I would fail. After all, my mind seemed to be telling me I wasn't athletic. I wasn't a fast runner. I wasn't supposed to win races! Kids like Willie Jenkins—cool kids—always won the races.

s I continued to run, I started talking to myself. "How can I get out of this race? You have to get out of this race, Herschel." And then, midway through the third lap, I stopped running. I just pulled up short, grabbed my leg, and started limping.

Rather than finish the race or just quit, I pretended that there was something wrong with my leg.

The coach came running over and asked me what was wrong. I told him that my leg was sore and that I was afraid that I would hurt it more if I kept running. I told him that I just *had* to stop running. Willie Jenkins won the race, of course.

I feel that that was the worst day I ever had in my life because I quit on myself. I don't think anyone else knew that I had faked the injury, but I felt bad afterward. I realized that I probably could have won that

race if I hadn't stopped running. Mostly, though, I felt bad because I hadn't given it an honest effort. I had given up.

'm not sure why I stopped running that day. I had never won a race before, so I guess I really didn't believe I could. Maybe I figured that I could save face by giving up before the race was over. That way, no one would ever know that I wasn't the fastest one; they might think that I would have won if I had kept running. Maybe I was just afraid of winning.

The biggest lesson I learned from my worst day is that no matter what happens along the way, you have to see things through to the end. Maybe I would have won that race if I had run my hardest all the way to the end, and maybe I wouldn't have won it. Either way, I would have felt a lot better about myself if I had at least completed it! My mother always told us to give 110 percent effort in whatever we do, and I knew I had not done that.

I also learned how much influence your mind has on how you perform. If you have ever competed, you

know that a lot goes on in your mind during a race or a game. Everyone has doubts about his abilities at times. That's what happened to me that day: I had never won a race before, so I didn't think I could do it. That day taught me that when you start thinking like that, you have to change gears. You have to persuade yourself that you *can* do it and start concentrating on giving it your best effort. Chances are you will find that you *can* do it, after all. Then, once you have had some success, it's easier to believe in yourself.

It was about a year after that race that I started working hard to become more athletic. I started playing football. I didn't really like the game, but I thought being on a team would help me make friends. And I kept running, although mostly, I raced my brother Lorenza and my older sister,

Veronica. She always beat me!

Instead of giving up, though, I went to the high school track coach and asked him how I could get bigger and stronger and faster. He told me to do push-ups, sit-ups, and run sprints. I did hundreds of exercises and sprints, and pretty soon I was winning races and scoring touchdowns.

I think my worst day taught me how important it is to give things a complete effort. Now, when I make a decision to do something, I give it 110 percent. I have never, ever quit on myself again. I learned how to prepare myself mentally—as well as physically—for a contest. And my experience over the years has shown me that hard work and following through on things do bring great results!

PHOTO CREDITS

Willie Anderson: *Andrew D. Bernstein / NBA Photos*

Brett Hull: *David E. Klutho / Sports Illustrated*

Dan Jansen: *Carl Yarbrough / Sports Illustrated*

Magic Johnson: *Bill Robbins / Sports Illustrated*

Shaun Jordan: *Heinz Kluetmeier / Sports Illustrated*

Jackie Joyner-Kersee: *Peter Read Miller / Sports Illustrated*

Julie Krone: *Heinz Kluetmeier / Sports Illustrated*

Greg LeMond: *Gianni Ciaccia*

Karl Malone: *Craig Molenhouse / Sports Illustrated*

Shirley Muldowney: *Richard Mackson / Sports Illustrated*

Martina Navratilova: *Melchior Digiacomo / Sports Illustrated*

Mary Decker Slaney: *Heinz Kluetmeier / Sports Illustrated*

Herschel Walker: *Bill Smith / Sports Illustrated*

ABOUT THE AUTHORS

Cathrine Wolf and Fred McMane live with their two daughters in Millburn, New Jersey. Cathrine is a senior editor at Sports Illustrated For Kids *magazine. Fred is the sports editor at* United Press International *and the co-author of several books on baseball. This is their first book together.*